30 MINUTE COOK

CW01506664

MY FOOD IS READY ALREADY?

Quick and Easy Recipes For All Dieters Packed With Protein and Nutrition While Low on Calories

Jose Tanner

Table of Contents

PART 1 9

Chapter 1: The Power of the Crock Pot and Its Benefits......................................10

Chapter 2: Healthy Breakfast Recipes...11

Boiled Eggs 11

One-Hour Bread 11

PART II...40

Chapter 3: Soups, Of Course! 50

Chapter 5: Tender Chicken..63

CHICKEN IN A POT 63

Layer the bottom of the cooker with the vegetables and top with the chicken parts. Mix the final components in a separate bowl and drizzle on top. Cook for 7-9 hours on low. 64

GOLDEN CHICKEN AND NOODLES..64

Mix together the first 6 ingredients. Place chicken parts in the cooker and top with the mixture. For 7-8 hours, cook on the low setting, until chicken juices run clear. Serve over noodles..65

Chapter 6: Flavorful Pork 74

Chapter 1: Mastering the Air Fryer 84

AF Buffalo Chicken Wings..100

Country Style Chicken Tenders..100

4)   Cook for ten minutes at 330°F and increase to 390°F for five minutes or until they are a nice golden brown...101

Beef Roll Ups 104

Yields: Four Servings...104

Chapter 5: Air Fryer Desserts 131

• AF Buffalo Chicken Wings...151

• Beef Roll Ups...152

Chapter 5: Air Fryer Desserts 153

Chapter 1: Keto Basics...156

Benefits of Increased Metabolism..156

Benefits of Cleansing..156

Chapter 2: Meal Plan Madness 158

Chapter 3: Breakfast Is For Champions 161

1. California Chicken Omelet..161

2. Steak and Eggs with Avocado 163

3. Pancakes an a Blender...164

4. Low Carb Smoothe Bowl 165

5. Feta and Pesto Omelet...166

6. Crepes with Cream and Raspberries 167

7. Green Monster Smoothie..169

Chapter 4: Lunch Crunch 170

1. Off The Cobb Salad 170

2. Avocado and Sardines..171

3. Chicken Salad A La Pesto 172

4. Bacon and Roasted Brussel Sprouts 173
5. Grilled Halloumi Salad 174
6. Bacon Broccoli Salad 175
7. Tuna Avocado Tartare 176
8. Warm Spinach and Shrimp 177
Chapter 5: Thinner by Dinner 179
1. Chicken Pad Thai 179
2. Chipotle Style Fish Tacos 181
3. Salmon with Avocado Lime Sauce 182
4. Siracha Lime Steak 183
5. Low Carb Sesame Chicken 184
6. Pan 'O Sausage 186
7. Quarter Pounder Keto Burger 188
BREAKFAST 190
Breakfast Recipes To Start Your Day Strong 190
Sconey Sconey Sunday – 6 SmartPoints Per Serving 190
3 Minute Breakfast Mug – 2 SmartPoints Per Serving 195
LUNCH RECIPES THAT WILL KEEP YOU SATISFIED ALL AFTERNOON. 197
Home Joe's Mediterranean Hummus With Pita Bread – 4 Smart Points Per Serving
.... 198
Ready in 30 Minutes 198
5 Minute Turkey Wrap – 8 SmartPoints Per Serving 200
Ready in 5 Minutes 200
Slow Cooker Southern Style Chicken Soup -4 SmartPoints Per Serving 201
Ready in 7 Hours 201
Healthy Zone Calzone – 4 SmartPoints Per Serving 203
Ready in 40 Minutes 203
8 Minute Tuna – 3 SmartPoints Per Serving 205
Ready in 8 Minutes 205
3 tablespoons of low-fat mayonnaise 205
Week-Long Rice With Chicken – 4 SmartPoints Per Serving 207
Ready in 30 Minutes 207
4 tablespoons of water 207
Admiral David's Broccoli – 5 SmartPoints Per Serving 209
Ready in 25 Minutes 209
DINNER RECIPES FOR THE HEALTHY BODY 211
Lightning Fast Curry Noodles – 3 SmartPoints Per Serving 211
Simple Season Chicken– 3 SmartPoints Per Serving 214
Homemade Multi-Purpose Marinara – 3 Smart Points Per Serving 216
Ready in 30 Minutes 216
Savory Grilled Salmon – 4 Smart Points Per Serving 218
Ready in 50 Minutes 218
Cheesy Baked Chicken – 5 SmartPoints Per Serving 220
Lean Mean Pork Chops – 3 SmartPoints Per Serving 222
Ready in 70 Minutes 222
Preheat the oven to 350 degrees F or 175 degrees C 222

Fast Cooking Scallops – 3 SmartPoints Per Serving.. 224
Ready in 20 Minutes.. 224

PART 1

Chapter 1: The Power of the Crock Pot and Its Benefits

The Ways You Can Benefit

Think of how many times you have experienced 'spells' that you did not feel like spending hours over the stove preparing dinner. Can you relate? How about the times during the holidays when you are planning on a houseful of guests; yikes? By the way, "Don't sweat it because you have your fabulous cooker and all of these new recipes to try out."

These are a few ways to make the path a bit easier:

Get Ahead of the Meal: Preparing food with your Crock-Pot® can put you ahead of the game the night before you have a busy day planned. You can always make the meal for the next day in just a few minutes. Put all of the ingredients (if they can combine overnight) into the pot, so when you get up the next morning; all you need to do is take it out of the fridge, and let it get to room temperature. Turn it on as you head out of the door and dinner will be ready when you get home. YES!

Save a lot of Effort and Time: All it takes is a few good recipes and a little bit of your valuable time. In most of the cases, these recipes are geared towards a fast lifestyle and will be ready with just a few simple steps. After some time and practice, you will know exactly which ones will be your favorites; all of them!

Cut Back on Dining Out: Having an enjoyable meal at home is so much more personal for your family because you (and your pot) prepared it! Not only that, You will eliminate the temptation to order foods that might not be so healthy and in turn—will be more expensive.

Watching the Extra Liquids: There is no need to use additional ingredients, other than what is described within each of the recipes. Ideally, you should not fill the more than half to two-thirds full of ingredients. Too much liquid will cause a leakage from the top and may result in improperly cooked food.

Cook it Slow & Leave it Alone: A slow cooker is known for creating delicious dishes while bringing out all of the natural flavors. So, go ahead and go to work or have some fun—or—better yet go to bed early! There is no need to worry about checking on it (unless the recipe calls for it). Each time the lid is removed—valuable heat is escaping—resulting in a breakdown of the advised times. Just keep that element it in mind, even though it smells so good!

Trimming the Fat: One huge advantage to the use of this type of cooking is you can save quite a chunk of money purchasing cheaper cuts of meat. Also, capitalize on the flavorful meat in small quantities and by bulking up on veggies with smaller meat portions.

Hot Antioxidants

Many recent studies have discovered cooking some food items such as tomatoes will increase the bioavailability of many of the nutrients. For example, lycopene which is linked to cancer and heart prevention becomes move available to the body because the heat releases the lycopene.

A study from 2003 compared the content of fresh, frozen, and canned corn which was processed with heat; specifically lutein and xeaxanthin, and found less lutein in the fresh version. This lutein is mostly well-known to protect you from some eye diseases.

Score 'ONE' for the Crock-Pot®.
Who Knew?

Basic Times & Settings

The question always arises of how long you should cook your items if you don't have a recipe for a Crock-Pot®. These are only general guidelines because the size of a pot will make a difference in the cooking times.

Regular Cooking Times	Crock Pot® High Temperatures	Crock Pot® Low Pot Temperatures
Hours		
1/4 to 1/2	1 to 2	4 to 6
1/2 to 1	2 to 3	5 to 7
1 to 2	3 to 4	6 to 8
2 to 4	4 to 6	8 to 12

Note: You must consider that root veggies take longer than other vegetables and meats which mean they should be placed in the lower part of the pot.
Are You Ready? Of course, you are!

Chapter 2: Healthy Breakfast Recipes

Boiled Eggs

Did you ever wake up in the middle of the night for a 'potty' break, and decided you want some boiled eggs or egg salad for breakfast or work tomorrow, but do not have the time to sit around and wait for the eggs to cook? You have a cure for that!
Ingredients and Instructions
The simplicity is amazing!

1) Pour some water into the Crock-Pot®, add as many eggs as you

want, and set the pot for 3 ½ hours on the low setting. Go back

to bed and enjoy tomorrow!

One-Hour Bread

Crave that fresh bread—no longer! You can have some delicious comfort food shortly!
Ingredients
1 ½ C. Baking Mix
3 Tbsp. Italian Seasoning

½ cup milk (skim is okay)
Optional: ½ C. shredded cheese or 3 Tbsp. Grated Parmesan cheese
Directions

1) Prepare the cooker with some non-stick cooking spray.

2) Combine all of the ingredients until the lumps are gone and

   empty into the cooker.

3) *Notes:* Bisquick® is a good choice.

Breakfast Fiesta Delight

Directions
1 Pound Country-Style Sausage
1 Package (28-ounces) frozen hash brown potatoes (thawed)
½ Cup whole milk
12 large eggs
1 ½ Cups shredded Mexican blend cheese
Directions

1) Prepare the Crock-Pot® by spraying it with some cooking spray

   to help with the cleanup.

2) Brown and crumble the sausage in a frying pan; remove and pat

   the grease away using a paper towel.

3) Whip the eggs together in a mixing container.

4) Layer the ingredients with a layer of potatoes, cheese, sausage,

   and eggs.

5) *Serving Time:* Have some salsa, sour cream, pepper, and salt for a

   tasty topping.

Servings: Six to Eight
Prep Time is fifteen minutes
Cooking Time is six to eight hours.
Italian Sausage Scramble
Ingredients

1 ½ Lbs. Italian sausage
1 medium yellow onion
6 medium red potatoes
¼ Cup fresh Italian minced parsley
One medium diced tomato
1 Cup frozen/fresh kernel corn
2 cups grated Cheddar cheese
Directions

1) Discard the outer casing from the sausage. Peel and dice the

   onions and potatoes.

2) Sauté the onion and crumbled sausage until browned. Place them

   on a few paper towels to absorb the grease/fat and add the items

   to the slow cooker.

3) Combine the rest of the ingredients—blending well. Cover and

   cook.

Servings: Six
Prep Time is 15 Minutes.
Cook Time: The high setting is for four hours, and the lower setting is for six to eight hours.

The Sweeter Side of Breakfast

Blueberry Steel Cut Oats

Ingredients
1 ½ C. of water
2 C. frozen blueberries
1 banana
1 C. Steel cut oats
1- ½ C. Vanilla almond milk
1 Tbsp. butter
1 ½ tsp. cinnamon
Directions

1) Prepare a six-quart cooker with the butter, making sure to cover

   the sides also.

2) Mash the banana slightly and add all of the ingredients into the Pot—stirring gently.

3) Place the top on the crock pot and cook for *one hour* on the HIGH setting; switch to the WARM setting overnight, and sleep tight!

Wake up ready for a busy day by adding a drizzle of honey and get moving!
Servings: Four to Six
Preparation Time: Fifteen Minutes
Cooking Time: Eight hours

Pumpkin Pie Oatmeal

Ingredients
1 C. oats (steel cut)
3 ½ C. water
1 C. pumpkin puree
¼ tsp. each:

- salt

- vanilla extract

- pumpkin pie spices

Optional: 2 Tbsp. maple syrup
Directions
1) Use some non-stick cooking spray to coat the Crock-Pot®.

2) Empty the oats into the Pot.

3) Mix the remainder of the ingredients in a large mixing container, and pour over the oats.

4) *Note*: If you like sweeter oatmeal just adjust the flavor after it is cooked.

Cooking Time: Eight hours on low

Pumpkin Butter
Ingredients
4 Cups pumpkin
1 tsp. ground ginger
2 tsp. cinnamon
1-¼ Cups honey/maple syrup
½ tsp. nutmeg
1 tsp. vanilla extract (*optional*)
Instructions

1) Blend the vanilla, syrup/honey, and pumpkin puree in the Crock-

   Pot®.

2) Cover and cook. During the last hour—add the ginger,

   cinnamon, and nutmeg.

3) If you want it a little thicker, you can crack the lid. After all, the

   aroma is tantalizing—especially first thing in the morning!

You can store in jars in the bottom of the fridge for a healthy addition—anytime.
Yields: About 10 ounces
Preparation Time: Five Minutes
Cooking Time: Five hours

Chapter 3: Time-Saving Lunch Specialties

Beef Tacos

Ingredients

1 Package taco seasoning

1 (ten-ounce) Can tomatoes and green chilies (Rotel)

1 Pound lean ground beef

Directions

1) Add everything listed into your Crock-Pot®.

2) If you are available; stir every couple of hours to break up the

beef or break it up before serving.

3) Serve on a floured tortilla or taco shell with your choice of

toppings.

Servings: 12 tacos

Preparation Time: Two Minutes

Cooking Time: Five to Six Hours

Root Beer & BBQ Chicken

Ingredients

1 (18-ounce) bottle barbecue sauce

4 chicken breasts

¼ teaspoon each pepper and salt

½ can or bottle root beer (full-sugar)

Note: You can use Dr. Pepper or Coke instead of root beer.

Directions

1) Pour the drink of choice, and place the chicken in the cooker.

2) Drain once the chicken has finished cooking, and discard most of

the liquid—but leaving enough to prevent dryness.

3) Flavor with some pepper and salt if desired and empty the

contents of the sauce into the Crock-Pot®, cooking for about 15

to 20 minutes.

4) Enjoy on some burger buns or rolls.

Cooking Time: The high temperature will have it ready in 3 hours.

Stuffed Banana Peppers

Ingredients
1 Package Italian Sausage
Banana Peppers
2 Jars of Marinara Sauce (approximately)

Directions
1) Adapt this for your crowd on the amounts used.

2) Remove both ends of the peppers and scoop out the seeds and discard them.

3) Pour ½ of the jar of sauce in the Crock-Pot®.

4) Dice the sausage, in case it is not already prepared.

5) Stuff the pepper with the sausage and put them into the Pot.

6) Pour the sauce over the banana peppers.

Cooking Time: Low for eight to nine hours

Crock-Pot® Taco Soup

Ingredients
1 (14.5-ounces) Can Each:
- Beef broth

- Petite diced tomatoes

1 (15-ounces) Can Each:
- Black beans

- Corn

1 (10-ounces) Can Rotel Original
1 Can kidney beans (16-ounces)
1 (1-oz.) pouch each:
- Taco seasoning mix

- Ranch seasoning mix (Hidden Valley)

½ teaspoon salt
1 ½ teaspoons onion powder
1 Lb. ground beef
Garnish: Sour Cream, Fritos, chopped green onions, or some shredded cheddar cheese
Notes: The recipe is excellent if you choose the 'Diced Tomatoes with Green Chilies.'
Directions

1) Cook the beef and drain. Rinse and drain all of the cans of

   veggies except for the chilies; reserve the liquid from the corn

   and tomatoes.

2) Toss everything into the Crock-Pot® (except for the garnishes).

3) Cook for the necessary time.

4) When the process is completed, add the garnishes of your choice

   with some Fritos on the side to complement the flavors

Servings: 8 to 10
Prep Time: Ten minutes
Cook Time: Low for 4 hrs. or High for 2 hrs.

Chapter 4: Dinner in a Hurry
Beef
Meat for the Tacos

Ingredients

2 Lbs. Ground beef (lean)

1 cup diced onions/Birds Eye Chopped Onions and Garlic

1 Package low-sodium taco seasoning mix

Directions

1) Put the burger into the Crock-Pot® and cook it for four to six

   hours. If you are in the area of the kitchen—stir the meat every

   couple of hours to ensure it is cooking evenly (if not—no

   worries).

2) When the cooking cycle is complete; drain the beef on some

   paper towels.

3) Combine the onions and ½ to one package of the taco seasoning.

4) Blend well and continue cooking for about one more hour

Servings: Six

Preparation Time: Five Minutes

Cooking Time: Low setting: Four to Six hours

Steak Pizzaiola

Ingredients

1 (one to two pounds) London Broil

1 Yellow, orange, or red sliced bell pepper

1 Large sliced onion

¼ Cup water

½ to ¾ of a jar (your choice) tomato pasta sauce

Directions

1) Flavor the meat with the pepper and salt and place it into the

   Crock-Pot®.

2) Add the peppers and onions, followed by your favorite sauce,

3) Cook for six to eight hours. (Flip a time or two if you are home.)

4) Serve over some pasta, potatoes, or veggies.

Cooking Time: Low heat for six to eight hours
Steaks in the Pot
Ingredients
4 to 6 steaks
¼ C. White Wine
2 T. A-1 Sauce
2 T. Dijon mustard
Directions
1) Blend the mustard and steak sauce; add it to each of the pieces of

steak.

2) Add the meat into the Crock-Pot®, add the wine, and cook for

six to eight hours.

Servings: Four or More
Cooking Time: 6 to 8 Hours on the low setting

Chicken and Turkey
Buffalo Chicken
Ingredients
3 to 5 Pounds (no skin or bones) chicken breasts
1 (12-ounce) Bottle Red Hot Wings Buffalo Sauce
1 Pouch ranch dressing mix
Directions
1) Put the chicken into the Crock-Pot®. Empty the sauce over the

breasts and sprinkle the ranch mix over the top. Cover and

Cook.

2) Take the chicken out of the Pot and throw away the sauce.

3) Shred the chicken with a couple of forks. It should be tender.

4) Put it back into the cooker and stir to coat the chicken

thoroughly.

5) Leave it in the pot on low about one more hour. Most of the

   sauce will be absorbed.

Cooking Time: Low for five hours
Caesar Chicken
Ingredients
1 bottle (12-ounces) Caesar dressing
4 skinless & boneless chicken breasts
½ Cup shredded Parmesan cheese
Directions

1) Add the breasts of chicken to the Crock-Pot®.

2) Cook the chicken for the specified time and drain the juices.

3) Empty the dressing over the breasts.

4) Sprinkle the cheese on top of that and cook for thirty more

   minutes covered until done.

Have a side of Caesar salad to complement the meal.
Servings: Four
Prep Time: 5 minutes
Cooking Time: Use the low setting for 6 hrs. ; the high setting High for 3 hrs.
Cranberry Chicken
Ingredients
4 (no skin or bones) Chicken Breasts
1 (8-ounces) bottle Kraft Catalina dressing
1 Pouch dry onion soup
1 (14-ounces) Can Ocean Spray Whole Cranberry Sauce
Directions

1) Cook the chicken in the Crock-Pot® according to your specified

   times. Drain the juices.

2) Combine the cranberry sauce, onion soup mix, and dressing.

   Empty it over the chicken.

3) Cook—covered—about 30 minutes.

Servings: Four

Preparation Time: Five minutes
Cooking Time: High for three hours or low for six hours
French Onion Chicken
Ingredients
4 Chicken breasts (no bones or skin)
1 Can French Onion soup (10.5-ounces)
½ cup sour cream
Directions

1) Put the breasts in the Pot and cook for the stated time. Empty

    the liquids.

2) Combine the soup and sour cream and add into the pot on top of

    the chicken

breasts.

3) Cook covered for about 30 minutes.

Servings: Four
Preparation Time: Five Minutes
Cooking Time: The high setting will take approximately three hours, whereas the low setting takes six hours.
Hawaiian Chicken
Ingredients
4 to 5 skinless and boneless breasts of chicken (thawed)
1 (20-oz.) Can Dole Pineapple Chunks
1 Bottle (12-oz.) Heinz Chili Sauce
1/3 C. brown sugar
Directions

1) Cook the chicken until its predetermined time limit is completed.

    Empty the liquid.

2) Combine the brown sugar, ½ of the juices of the can of

    pineapples, the chili sauce, and the chunks of pineapple.

3) Empty the mixture over the drained breasts and heat on the high

    setting for approximately 30 minutes or so.

4) Have a bit of pineapple in every bite. Yummy!

Servings: 4 to 5
Preparation Time: 5 min.
Cooking Time: High = 6 hrs. / Low = 3 hrs.
Honey Mustard Chicken
Ingredients
1 (12-ounces) Bottle Dijon mustard
1/3 C. honey
4 skinless & boneless chicken breasts (thawed)
Directions

1) Cook the chicken for its predetermined time and dispose of the

   juices.

2) Combine the mustard and honey in a small dish.

3) Empty the sauce over the chicken and cook for about ½ hour

   (covered) until done,

Servings: Four
Preparation Time: Five Minutes
Cooking Time: Use the low setting for six hrs. Or on high for three hrs.
Chicken Italian Style
Ingredients
4 chicken breasts (thawed – no bones- no skin)
1 (16-ounce) Bottle Italian Dressing
Directions

1) Place the breasts of chicken into your Crock-Pot® and pour the

   dressing on them.

2) Put the lid on and let it do your work!

Servings: Four
Preparation Time: 5 minutes
Cooking Time: Use the high setting to prepare the chicken for 3.5 hrs. Or use the low setting for 7 hours.
Swedish Meatballs
Ingredients
1 (12-ounce) jar Heinz HomeStyle Gravy (Savory Beef)
1 (eight-ounce) container of sour cream
1 Bag Frozen Meatballs
Instructions

1) Empty the gravy into the Crock-Pot®, followed by the sour cream.

2) Combine these until they are completely blended.

3) Toss the package of frozen meatballs into the Pot filling to approximately 2/3 to ¾ of the space.

4) Place the lid on the pot and cook—occasionally stirring if you happen to be close to the kitchen.

5) You can always make more or less of the recipe depending on how many people you will serve.

Cooking Time: Low for a minimum of 5 hours
Sweet and Sour Chicken
Ingredients
1 (22-ounces) Bag frozen Tyson Chicken Breast
2 Cups cooked rice/steamed vegetables (or both)
1 bottle (18-ounces) Apricot Preserves
1 jar (12-ounces) chili sauce
Directions
1) Layer the frozen chicken pieces into the Crock-Pot®.

2) Combine the preserves and chili sauce in a small container (a mixing cup is ideal). Empty it over the chicken. *Note:* You can also use pineapple or a combination.

3) Toss to mix and let the Pot do the work.

4) Enjoy with some veggies and rice.

Servings: Six (one cup per serving)
Cooking Time on the high setting is 2 to 3 hours.
Creamy Taco Chicken
Ingredients

1 Can Rotel Original Tomatoes with Green Chilies
3 chicken breasts (no bone or skin)
4-ounces cream cheese (regular or light)
Directions

1) Pour the tomatoes, and place the chicken into the slow cooker.

2) A few minutes before the end of the cooking cycle, use a fork or tongs to shred the chicken.

3) Put the cream cheese on top of the mixture, but don't stir.

4) By the time the meal is ready, the cheese will be oozing into your chicken. Yummy!

Suggestions: You can use this in a casserole, over rice, as a salad, or any other creative plan you may have for your meal.
Cooking Time: Low temperature - Six to Eight hours

Stuffed – Roasted Turkey

Ingredients
2 C. Stuffing Mix
Black pepper and salt
6 Pounds Turkey
1 Tablespoon melted butter
Instructions

1) Use the package instructions to prepare the stuffing.

2) Flavor the turkey with some melted butter, pepper, and salt.

3) Prepare the bird by loosely placing the stuffing in the carcass.

4) Cover and let the Pot do the rest.

Servings: Four
Cooking Time: Low: 9 to 11 hours; High: 5 hours

Fish

Citrus Flavored Fish

Ingredients
Pepper and Salt
1 ½ pounds fish fillets
1 medium chopped onion
4 tsp. oil
5 Tbsp. Chopped parsley
2 tsp. Each grated: lemon and orange rind

Garnish: Lemon and orange slices
Directions
Use some butter to grease the Crock-Pot®.

1) Flavor the fish with some pepper and salt and put it into the pot.

2) Add the parsley, grated rinds, and onion as well as the oil over the fish.

3) Cover and cook.

4) When ready to eat; garnish with some lemon or orange slices.

Cooking Time: 1 ½ Hours on Low
Salmon Bake
Ingredients
3 (one-pound) Cans Salmon
1 (16-ounces) can tomato puree
4 cups bread crumbs (10 slices worth)
1 chopped green pepper
3 teaspoons lemon juice
2 crushed chicken bouillon cubes
1 Can each (condensed) cream of onion soup & cream of celery soup
6 (well-beaten) eggs
½ cup milk
Directions

1) Use some cooking spray or other oil to grease the Crock-Pot® lightly.

2) Blend all of the ingredients—except for the milk and celery soup into the Pot.

3) Cover and cook.

4) Combine and stir the milk and celery soup in a small pan to use as a sauce for the salmon.

5) When the salmon is done, garnish and enjoy with the special

   sauce!

Cooking Time: High for three hours or low for four to six hours

Pork
BBQ Style Pork Steaks
Ingredients
4 (½-inch cut) Pork shoulder steaks
2 large sliced tomatoes
1 large onion
1 large thinly sliced bell pepper
1 Tbsp. Each:

- Vegetable oil

- Tapioca (quick-cooking)

¼ C. red wine
½ tsp. cumin
½ C. barbecue sauce (your choice)
Directions
1) Slice and cut the onion as if you are preparing to make onion

   rings for dinner.

2) Trim away an excess fat and slice the steaks in half - lengthwise.

3) Brown the steaks in skillet using hot oil, and drain on paper

   towels.

4) Organize the peppers, tomatoes, and onions in the Crock-Pot®;

   sprinkling the tapioca over them. Place the pork in last.

5) Prepare the cumin, wine, and barbecue sauce in a small dish. Pour

   it over the ingredients in the Pot, and cover.

Servings: Four
Cooking Time: Low Heat – Six to Eight Hours (or until veggies and meat are tender)

Note: The recipe is based on a 3 ½- or a 4-quart Crock-Pot®. If you have a different size the cooking time may vary.

Pepsi® Roast

Ingredients

1 Can Cream of mushroom soup

5 Lb. Pork Roast/ Steak/Chops

½ package dry onion soup mix

1 can Regular Pepsi (Don't use Diet)

Directions

1) Put the meat in the Crock-Pot® first and sprinkle with the soup

   mix.

2) Empty the mushroom soup and Pepsi over the meat.

3) Close the lid and let the pot do the rest of the chore.

Suggestion: Use the sauce to pour over some rice or potatoes.

Servings: Eight

Cooking Time: Low setting for six to seven hours

Ranch Chops

Ingredients

Pouch – Ranch Dressing Mix

Pork Chops

1 Can Cream of Chicken Soup Plus (+) 1 Can Water OR 2 Cups Cream of Chicken

Directions

1) Pour the liquids into the Crock-Pot® along with the chops and

   dressing mix.

Cooking Time: Use the low-temperature setting for four to six hours.

Ham in Cider Gravy

This ham is so tasty it cannot remain in the 'breakfast only' slot. It is so tasty and can advance to lunch and dinner menus as well.

Ingredients

1 (one to four pound) Ham

¾ cup maple syrup

2 cups unsweetened apple cider

3 Tablespoons cornstarch

Directions

1) Arrange the ham in the Crock-Pot® and top it off with the syrup

   and cider.

2) Cook until the time indicated below is completed.

3) Move the ham to a serving platter. Pour the liquid into a large cup (a measuring cup is perfect).

4) Whisk ½ of the cider and the cornstarch on the stovetop using the low-temperature setting until it is smooth. Continue whisking and increase the burner to med-low—adding small amounts of cider at a time—until the gravy is bubbly and thickened to the desired consistency.

Servings: Four to Eight
Preparation Time: Four minutes
Cooking Time: Low - six to eight hours

Casseroles

Crock-Pot® Dinner: Beef or Chicken

Ingredients
1 Whole/cut up chicken –or- legs and thighs OR a Beef Roast
2 Carrots
4 Potatoes
5 Ounces water
1 Can celery or cream of mushroom soup (10 ¾ ounce)
Directions

1) Cut the carrots into four-inch chunks. Put all of the ingredients into the Crock-Pot®.

2) Set the Pot and let it 'go.'

Servings: Four
Cooking Time: The high setting will cook the meal in six hours, or you can cook it all day using the low-temperature setting.

Squash 'N Chops

Ingredients
5 Pork (boneless) Port cutlets or chops
2 medium oranges
1 ¼ Pounds delicate/butternut squash
1/8 tsp. Ground red pepper

½ tsp. Garlic salt

¼ tsp. Each: Ginger, cloves, and cinnamon

Directions

1) Peel and slice the oranges. Peel and slice the squash lengthwise and discard the seeds. Cut the 'half' into sections ½-inches thick.

2) Flavor the pork with some garlic salt and red peppers. Use a 4- to 5- quart Crock-Pot® and place the chops/cutlets in the bottom.

3) Combine the ginger, cinnamon, and cloves in a small dish.

4) Top off the pork with the oranges along with the toppings in step 3.

5) Cover and cook.

Servings: 5

Cooking Time: Low for 4 hours

Lasagna Enchantment

This one has a few more steps, but it is so worth it—and it's easy.

Ingredients

2 Cans diced tomatoes (28-ounces) drained

Four finely chopped clove of garlic

2 Tbsp. oregano

½ tsp. salt

15-ounces fresh ricotta

¼ tsp. pepper

½ tsp. salt

½ C. shredded Parmesan cheese

1 (12-ounce) Package uncooked lasagna noodles

½ tsp. fresh (finely chopped) parsley – more if desired

2 C. spinach leaves (bagged is okay)

2 C. shredded Mozzarella cheese

Directions

1) Mix the garlic, drained tomatoes, pepper, salt, and oregano in a mixing container.

2) In another bowl, blend the parsley, Parmesan, and ricotta cheese.

3) Dip anywhere from 1/3 to ½ cup of the tomato combination on the base of the Crock-Pot®.

4) Layer the noodles, spinach, several dollops of the ricotta combo, and 1/3 to about ½ of the tomato combination. Sprinkle the mozzarella on the top of that section. Continue the process with the mozzarella on the top.

5) Close the lid on the Pot and let it do the work.

Servings: Six to Eight
Prep Time: 20 Minutes
Cook Time: High is 2 Hrs. or Low is 3 to 4 Hrs.

Sweet Potato Casserole

Ingredients
1 ½ C. applesauce
1 tsp. ground cinnamon
3 Tbsp. Margarine/butter
½ C. Toasted chopped nuts
2/3 C. Brown sugar
6 medium sweet potatoes

Directions
1) Peel and slice the potatoes cutting them into ½-inch bits and drop them into a 3 ½-quart Crock-Pot®.

2) In a separate dish, mix the brown sugar, cinnamon, melted butter, and applesauce. *Note*: Be sure you pack the brown sugar tight when it is measured.

3) Empty the mixture over the potatoes in the Pot.

4) When the potatoes are tender; you can top with the chopped nuts. Yummy!

Cooking Time: Six to Eight hours
Sides/Veggies
Slow Cooked Baked Potatoes
Ingredients
6 Baking Potatoes
Kosher Salt
Oil
Garnishes: Your choice
Directions
1) Prepare the potatoes with a good scrub and rinsing, but do not

   dry them.

2) Put each one in some foil while poking holes in each one using a

   fork.

3) Use a small amount of oil to drizzle over each one adding a

   sprinkle of salt, and close the foil.

4) To keep them from getting soggy, ball up several wads of foil

   into the cooker.

5) Layer the potatoes on the balls and cover. Leave them on warm

   in the Crock-Pot® until ready to serve.

Cooking Time: Low – Six to Eight Hours
Corn on the Cob
Ingredients
3 ears or 5 to 6 halves – Corn on the cob
Salt as needed
1/2 stick or ¼ cup of softened butter
Directions
1) Shuck and remove the silks from the corn; break them into

   halves.

2) Cover each one with butter and wrap individually in foil.

3) Wad some foil balls up in the base of the unit and add about 1-inch of water.

4) Put the potatoes into the Crock-Pot®, and cook for the allotted time.

Servings: 4
Preparation Time: Five minutes
Cooking Time: Use the high setting for two hours. *Note*: The cooking time may vary if you prepare the corn with another unit besides a 5 to 6-quart pot.

Ranch Mushrooms
Ingredients
½ Cup Melted butter
1 Pound fresh mushrooms
1 Package - ranch salad dressing mix
Instructions
1) Leave the mushrooms whole and wash them well.

2) Put them into the Crock-Pot®, adding the oil and ranch mix by drizzling it over the mushrooms.

3) Cover the Pot. It is best to stir once after hour one to blend the butter.

Servings: Six
Cooking Time: Low will have your mushrooms ready in three to four hours.

Sweet Potatoes
Ingredients
4 medium sweet potatoes
Optional Garnishes:
Brown Sugar, Butter, Mini Marshmallows
Directions
1) Clean and prepare the potatoes—thoroughly dry.

2) Use a fork and poke holes in each one, and double wrap them in aluminum foil.

3) Put them in the Crock-Pot®--cooking them the specified amount of time. If you are close to the kitchen; turn and flip the potatoes in the pot occasionally.

4) Once they are done, add the garnishes of your choice and serve.

Servings: Four
Preparation Time: Five Minutes
Cooking Time: The Low setting is used for 8 hrs. or the High setting for 4 hrs. (Times may vary depending on the size of the potatoes, but you will know when they are ready by how soft the potato is when you give it a squeeze.)

Chapter 5: Desserts – Snacks & Treats to Devour

Apple Dump Cake

Ingredients
Butter (1 Stick)
Yellow cake mix (1 box)
Apple pie filling (1 Can)
Directions

1) Empty the apple filling into the Crock-Pot®.

2) *Dump* in the mix and then the butter on top of the mix.

Cooking Time: Cook the cake in the Pot on the low setting for approximately four hours for best results.
Enjoy!

Applesauce

Ingredients
12 Apples
1 teaspoon juice (+) ¼ of the lemon peel
2 cinnamon sticks
Directions

1) Peel, core, and slice the apples. Put the apples, lemon peel, and sticks into the Crock-Pot®.

2) Provide a drizzle to the top with the juice and set the cooking timer.

3) When the treat is ready—throw the lemon peel and cinnamon sticks into the garbage.

4) Blend with a regular or immersion blender.

5) Chill for a few hours.

Cooking Time is five to seven hrs.

Peach Cobbler

Ingredients

1 White cake mix (not prepared)
6 Large peaches
1- Stick (½- Cup) softened butter

Directions

1) Peel and slice the peaches, and put them into the Crock-Pot®.

2) Blend the butter and cake mix using a pastry blender. You want a crumbly texture.

3) Sprinkle the mix over the peaches, and cook.

Enjoy with a bowl of ice cream.

Servings: Eight

Preparation Time: Fifteen minutes

Cooking Times on the high setting is two to three hours; whereas the Low cycle will extend for about four hours.

Cocktail Franks – Sweet and Sour

Ingredients

40- Ounces Pineapple chunks
2 Pounds cocktail franks
1 Cup each:

- Grape jelly

- Chili sauce

3 Tablespoons each:

- Prepared mustard

- Lemon juice

Directions

1) Mix the jelly, chili sauce, mustard, and lemon juice in the Pot, mixing it well.

2) Cover and use the high setting for fifteen to twenty minutes to blend the ingredients

3) Slice the franks into bite-sized pieces and add to the Crock-Pot®.

4) Pour in the drained chunks of pineapple.

Servings: 10
Cooking Times: *High* setting for two hours; *Low* setting for four hours.

Index for the Recipes
Chapter 2: Healthy Breakfast Recipes

- Boiled Eggs

- One-Hour Bread

- Breakfast Fiesta Delight

- Italian Sausage Scramble

The Sweeter Side of Breakfast
- Blueberry Steel Cut Oats

- Pumpkin Pie Oatmeal

- Pumpkin Butter

Chapter 3: Time-Saving Lunch Specialties

- Beef Tacos

- Root Beer & BBQ Chicken

- Stuffed Banana Peppers

- Crock-Pot® Taco Soup

Chapter 4: Dinner in a Hurry
Beef
- Meat for the Tacos

- Steak Pizzaiola

- Steak in the Pot

Chicken & Turkey
- Buffalo Chicken

- Caesar Chicken

- Cranberry Chicken

- French Onion Chicken

- Hawaiian Chicken

- Honey Mustard Chicken

- Chicken Italian Style

- Swedish Meatballs

- Sweet and Sour Chicken

- Creamy Taco Chicken

- Stuffed – Roasted Turkey

Fish
- Citrus Flavored Fish

- Salmon Bake

Pork
- BBQ Style Pork Steaks

- Pepsi® Roast

- Ranch Chops

- Ham in Cider Gravy

Casseroles
- Crock-Pot® Dinner: Beef or Chicken

- Squash 'N Chops

- Lasagna Enchantment

- Sweet Potato Casserole

Sides & Veggies
- Slow Cooked Baked Potatoes

- Corn on the Cob

- Ranch Mushrooms

- Sweet Potatoes

Chapter 5: Desserts to Devour
- Apple Dump Cake

- Applesauce

- Peach Cobbler

- Cocktail Franks – Sweet and Sour

PART II

Chapter 1: Just For Starters

Do you have a party you want to bring a dish to? Maybe you just need a side dish to go along with a meal. Either way, the following recipes are great additions to any event or meal.

TACO DIP

5-7 hours in the slow cooker

Yields about 7 cups

14 ½ ounce can of tomatoes, stewed

15 ounce can of black beans, drained and washed

15 ¼ ounce can of corn, drained

1 taco seasoning envelope

8 ounce can of tomato sauce

16 ounce can of kidney beans, washed and drained

4 ounce can of green chilies, chopped

¾ cup(s) of chopped onion

Tortilla chips

Place everything into the slow cooker, excluding for the chips, then cook for 5-7 hours on low. Serve with Tortilla Chips.

MAC AND CHEESE

4 ½ hours in the slow cooker

Yields about 10 servings

16 ounce package of elbow macaroni

12 ounce can of evaporated milk

½ cup(s) of melted butter

1 cup(s) of milk

10 ¾ ounce can of cheddar cheese soup

2 beaten eggs

4 cup(s) of of cheddar cheese, shredded and divided

1/8 teaspoon(s) paprika

Make the noodles in accordance with the package directions and drain. Put pasta and butter into the slow cooker. Next, in a separate bowl mix the milk, soup, evaporated milk, eggs, and 3 cups of the cheese together. Pour the mixture in the cooker, stirring well. Cook for at least 4 hours on low. Lastly, add in what cheese and paprika is left and cook further until all is melted.

WILD RICE WITH MUSHROOMS

7-8 hours in the slow cooker

Yields about 12-15 servings

½ cup(s) of butter

1 cup(s) of brown rice

3-4 ounce cans of mushrooms

2 ¼ cup(s) of water

10 ½ ounce can of beef consommé

1 cup(s) of wild rice

10 ½ ounce can of French onion soup

Mix all ingredients in the cooker. Cook for 7-8 hours on the low setting.

CRAB DIP

3-4 hours in the slow cooker

Yields about 5 cups

1/3 cup(s) of salsa

½ cup(s) of milk

4 ounce can of chilies, chopped

3 packages of cubed cream cheese

1 cup(s) of of green onions, sliced thinly

2-8 ounce packages of real or imitation crab, flaked

Crackers

Coat slow cooker with nonstick spray and dump in milk and salsa. Mix until blended and add the remaining ingredients except for the crackers. Cook for 3-4 hours on low. Stir and serve on crackers.

PARTY BEANS

5-7 hours in the slow cooker

Yields about 14-16 servings

15 ½ ounce can of great northern beans, washed and drained

1/8 teaspoon(s) pepper

1 teaspoon(s) ground mustard

2 bay leaves

½ cup(s) of water

2-3 tablespoon(s) cider vinegar

½ cup(s) of brown sugar packed

1 chopped green pepper

1 chopped onion

1 chopped sweet red pepper

1 ½ cup(s) of ketchup

16 ounce can of kidney beans, washed and drained

15 ½ ounce can of black-eyed peas, washed and drained

15 ounce can of black beans, washed and drained

15 ounce can of lima beans, washed and drained

Combine everything into the slow cooker. Cooke for 5-7 hours on low. Remove bay leaves and serve.

CHILI CHEESE SAUCE

45 minutes in the slow cooker

Yields about 20 servings

2-15 ounce cans of chili (no beans)

2 lb. brick of cheese, cubed

16 ounce jar of picante sauce

2-8 ounce packages of cream cheese

Mix everything into slow cooker. Cook for 45 minutes until everything is melted, mixed well, and warmed through. Serve with tortilla chips.

Chapter 2: Sandwiches That Will Melt in Your Mouth

These sandwiches or excellent for lunches, events and quick dinners! They will melt in your mouth and are sure to get you recipe requests.

BBQ CHICKEN SANDWICHES

6-8 hours in the slow cooker

Yields about 8-10 servings

6 cup(s) of of cooked, diced or shredded chicken

1 cup(s) of diced onion

1 ¼ cup(s) of ketchup

¼ cup(s) of brown sugar, packed

1 teaspoon(s) salt

¼ teaspoon(s) hot pepper sauce

¼ cup(s) of Worcestershire sauce

¼ cup(s) of cider vinegar or red wine vinegar

1 teaspoon(s) celery seed

2 cup(s) of water

1 teaspoon(s) chili powder

Buns

Merge all the components into the cooker except the buns and cook it for 6-8 hours on the low setting. Provide warm or toasted buns.

RANCH CHICKEN SANDWICHES

6-8 hours in the slow cooker

Yields about 6 servings

8 ounce of bacon bits

2 lbs. of chicken breasts, boneless

2 envelopes of dry Ranch seasoning

2-8 ounce blocks of cream cheese

Put the chicken, cheese and ranch into the cooker and it should cook for 6-8 hours on the low setting. Shred the chicken in the slow cooker with two forks, stir in the bacon bits and serve on warm or toasted buns.

HAM SANDWICHES

4-5 hours in the slow cooker

Yields about 12 servings

2 cup(s) of apple juice

½ sweet pickle relish

1 teaspoon(s) paprika

2 teaspoon(s) mustard

3 lbs. or about 40 slices of ham, sliced thin

Buns

2/3 cup(s) of brown sugar

Relish

Join the initial five ingredients in to a bowl. Layer the ham into the bottom of the slow cooker and then pour sauce on it. Cook for at least 4-5 hours on the low setting and serve on warm buns.

BEEF SANDWICHES

6-8 hours in the slow cooker

Yields about 8-10 servings

1 boneless chuck roast that is about 3-4 lbs.

¼ teaspoon(s) cayenne pepper

1 teaspoon(s) marjoram

1 teaspoon(s) caraway seeds

1 teaspoon(s) celery seed

2 teaspoon(s) garlic powder

2 teaspoon(s) oregano

2 teaspoon(s) salt

1 tablespoon(s) minced onion

1 teaspoon(s) rosemary

Buns

Mix all the seasonings and rub all over the entire roast. For 6-8 hours, cook on the low setting. Shred using two forks and serve on warm or toasted buns.

MEATBALL SUBS

6-8 hours in the slow cooker

Yields about 6 servings

1 cup(s) of milk

3 tablespoon(s) onion, chopped

¾ oats, quick-cooking

1 ½ teaspoon(s) salt

1 ½ lbs. ground beef

2 tablespoon(s) sugar

1 cup(s) of ketchup

3 tablespoon(s) vinegar

½ cup(s) of water

Buns

Provolone cheese

Break up meat into a bowl and combine with the first 4 ingredients. Roll meat into 1 inch balls and set all of them into a slow cooker. Grab a separate bowl and in it, combine, join the sugar, vinegar, ketchup, and water, then drizzle onto meatballs. For at least 6-8 hours, cook on the low setting and serve on toasted buns with or without cheese.

Chapter 3: Soups, Of Course!

No cookbook would be complete without some savory soups, especially a slow cooker book! Throw these together during a bitter winter day and warm up when you get home.

VEGETABLE SOUP

8 hours in the slow cooker

Yields about 8-10 servings

3 cup(s) of water

14 ½ ounce can of diced tomatoes, with liquid

1 lb. boneless round steak, cubed

2 potatoes, cubed

3 ribs of celery, sliced

1 large onion diced

2 carrots, sliced

½ cup(s) of corn

½ cup(s) of beans

½ cup(s) of peas

½ teaspoon(s) basil

¼ teaspoon(s) pepper

½ teaspoon(s) oregano

½ teaspoon(s) salt

3 cubes of beef bouillon

Mix everything into the slow cooker and then cook for about 8 hours on high.

TROUT CHOWDER

2 hours in the slow cooker

Yields about 6 servings

2 cup(s) of milk

1 cup(s) of cubed Monterey Jack cheese

¼ teaspoon(s) garlic powder

1 cup(s) of ranch salad dressing

10 ounce thawed package of frozen broccoli

1 lb. Trout filets with the skin removed (or some other white fish favorite)

1 tablespoon(s) butter

1 chopped medium onion

1 cup(s) of cubed cheddar cheese

Paprika

Place the first seven ingredients into the slow cooker and mix. Sauté the chopped onion in the butter and then toss it into the slow cooker. Next, cook for 2 hours on the high setting. When the dish is finished, the fish will flake very easily. Sprinkle each serving with some Paprika and serve with crackers or bread.

BUFFALO CHICKEN SOUP

4-5 hours in the slow cooker

Yields about 8 servings

3 cup(s) of cooked chicken

1/8 cup(s) of hot pepper sauce

6 cup(s) of milk

1 cup(s) of sour cream

3 10 ¾ ounce cans of cream of chicken soup

Join all the components into the cooker and for 4-5 hours, cook on the low setting.

WHITE CHILI

8-10 hours in the slow cooker

Yields about 12 servings

4 minced garlic cloves

2 chopped medium onions

1 teaspoon(s) salt

2 chicken bouillon cubes

½ teaspoon(s) ground cloves

2 teaspoon(s) oregano

2-4 ounce cans of green chilies

1 tablespoon(s) cumin

½-1 teaspoon(s) cayenne pepper

2 qt. of water

3 lbs. of boneless chicken without the skin

1 lb. dry navy beans

Shredded Monterey Jack cheese

Sour Cream

Chives, chopped

Put the garlic and onions into the cooker first and then put the remaining ingredients except the cheese, sour cream, and chives. For at least 8-10 hours, cook on the high setting. Stir and shred meat then serve with toppings of cheese, sour cream, and chives.

POTATO SOUP

7-8 hours in the slow cooker

Yields about 8-10 servings

5 cup(s) of water

¼ teaspoon(s) pepper

2 teaspoon(s) salt

¼ cup(s) of butter

4 teaspoon(s) chicken bouillon

½ celery, chopped

½ carrots, thinly sliced

2 cup(s) of onion, chopped

6 cup(s) of potatoes, cubed with or without skins

3 tablespoon(s) parsley

12 ounce can of evaporated milk

Chives, chopped

Place the first nine ingredients into the cooker and for at least 7-8 hours, cook on high. Include the parsley and milk, then stir. Continue cooking for an additional 30-60 minutes. Sprinkle chives on top.

Chapter 4: Juicy Beef

These recipes feature mouthwatering beef and common ingredients to make a meal everyone will love!

ITALIAN ROAST

8-9 hours in the slow cooker

Yields about 8-10 servings

½-1 teaspoon(s) salt

½ teaspoon(s) garlic powder

¼ teaspoon(s) pepper

1 boneless rump roast at around 3 ½ lbs.

1 diced medium onion

4 ½ ounce drained can of mushrooms

¼-1/2 cup(s) of beef broth or red wine

14 ounce jar of spaghetti sauce

Cooked Noodles

Merge the first 3 seasonings into a bowl and cut the roast in half. Rub the seasoning all over the roast and put it in the slow cooker. Top with the onions and mushrooms. Mix wine or broth with the spaghetti sauce and pour over everything in cooker. Cook for at least 8-9 hours on the low setting and serve.

CORNED BEEF AND CABBAGE

8-9 hours in the slow cooker

Yields about 6-8 servings

1 lb. baby carrots

4 potatoes, quartered with or without skin

1 medium onion, cut into large chunks

½ teaspoon(s) pepper

1 bay leaf

3 minced garlic cloves

2 tablespoon(s) cider vinegar

2 tablespoon(s) sugar

3 cup(s) of water

1 small head of cabbage sliced into chunks

1 corned beef brisket, about 3 pounds, with a spice packet

Put the first 3 ingredients into the cooker. Merge the water and spices into a separate bowl and pour into cooker. On top of the contents of the cooker, add your cabbage and brisket. Once all is in the cooker, cook for at least 8-9 hours on low. Remove bay leaf and serve.

SMOKEY BEEF AND BEANS

6-7 hours in the slow cooker

Yields about 8 servings

1 cup(s) of onion, chopped

1 lb. ground beef

¼ teaspoon(s) pepper

½ teaspoon(s) salt

1 teaspoon(s) liquid smoke

¼ cup(s) of brown sugar, packed

16 ounce can of drained and washed kidney beans

16 ounce can of drained butter beans

3 tablespoon(s) vinegar

2-16 ounce cans of beans and pork

1 cup(s) of ketchup

12 strips of cooked and crumbled bacon

Cook beef and onions until the beef is no longer pink in a skillet. Combine beef and onions and remaining components into the cooker and cook 6-7 hours on the low setting.

CHILI MAC

6 hours in the slow cooker

Yields about 12 servings

1 envelope chili seasoning

2 chopped green peppers

1 chopped onion

1 lb. ground beef

4 chopped celery ribs

8 ounce can of tomato sauce

2-15 ounce cans of hot chili beans with the liquid

7 ounce package of elbow macaroni

2 minced garlic cloves

Salt and Pepper

Mix the first 8 components into the cooker. For 6 hours, cook on low. Cook the noodles according to the package, drain and then stir into the chili. Serve warm with pepper and salt.

MUSHROOM BEEF OVER NOODLES

8 hours in the slow cooker

Yields about 6-8 servings

7.5 cans of French onion soup

7.5 cans of golden mushroom soup

¼ cup(s) of seasoned bread crumbs

10 ¾ cans of beefy mushroom soup

2 lbs. of beef stew meat, cubed

12 ounce package of wide egg noodles

Mix together the soups and bread crumbs right in the slow cooker, then add the beef. Cook for at least 8 hours on the low setting. Cook the noodles in accordance with the package directions and drain. Serve over noodles.

CASSEROLE THAT COOKS ITSELF

6-8 hours in the slow cooker

Yields about 12 servings

1 cup(s) of wild rice, rinsed

1 cup(s) of carrots, chopped

1 minced garlic clove

1 cup(s) of celery, chopped

2-4 ounce cans of drained mushrooms

1 chopped onion

3 beef bouillon cubes

½ cup(s) of slivered almonds

2 lbs. cubed boneless round steak

2 ½ teaspoon(s) season salt

3 cup(s) of water

Put ingredients into the slow cooker from the top of the list to the bottom, and do not stir. For 6-8 hours, cook on low. Stir and serve.

SPICY GOULASH

5-6 hours in the slow cooker

Yields about 12 servings

2-16 ounce jars of drained kidney beans

1 chopped onion

4-14 ¼ ounce cans of Mexican diced tomatoes with the liquid

2 cup(s) of water

1 lb. ground beef

2 tablespoon(s) chili powder

1 chopped green pepper

¼ cup(s) of red wine vinegar

1 tablespoon(s) Worcestershire sauce

1 teaspoon(s) basil

2 teaspoon(s) beef bouillon

1 teaspoon(s) parsley

¼ teaspoon(s) pepper

1 teaspoon(s) cumin

2 cup(s) of uncooked elbow macaroni

Cook beef in a pan until it is no longer pink. While it's cooking, place all other ingredients into the slow cooker, except noodles. Stir in cooked beef and cook for 5 hours on low. Stir in noodles for another 30 minutes and serve when the noodles are tender.

GOLOMBKI

6-8 hours in the slow cooker

Yields about 8 servings

1 lb. ground beef

1 cup(s) of converted rice, uncooked

1 small chopped onion

½ teaspoon(s) sugar

1 cup(s) of water

¾ teaspoon(s) salt

24 ounce jar of meatless spaghetti sauce

2-10 ¾ ounce tomato soup

¼ teaspoon(s) pepper

1 medium head of chopped cabbage

Cook onions and beef in a pan until no longer pink. Mix in salt, pepper, and rice. In separate bowl, combine sugar, water, spaghetti, and soup. In the slow cooker place 1/3 of the sauce mixture, ½ of the beef mixture and 1/3 of the cabbage. Repeat once, then dump in the rest of the sauce and remaining cabbage. For 6-8 hours, cook on low. Serve when rice is cooked.

SLOW COOKED MEAT LOAF

5-6 hours in the slow cooker

Yields about 6 servings

2/3 cup(s) of seasoned bread crumbs

½ teaspoon(s) rubbed sage

½ teaspoon(s) Worcestershire sauce

2 eggs

1 teaspoon(s) salt

¾ cup(s) of milk

2 teaspoon(s) minced onion

2 tablespoon(s) brown sugar

1½ lb. ground beef

¼ cup(s) of ketchup

1 teaspoon(s) ground mustard

Mix together the first 6 ingredients in a bowl, then stir in the ground beef well. Make into a loaf and for 5-6 hours, cook on low in the slow cooker. In a different dish blend the remaining of the components and drizzle over the loaf. Cook for an additional 15 minutes and serve.

SLOW COOKER PIZZA

3 hours in the slow cooker

Yields about 6-8 servings

¼ cup(s) of chopped onion

4 ½ ounce can of drained mushrooms

26 ounce jar of spaghetti sauce

1 ½ teaspoon(s) Italian seasoning

3 cup(s) of shredded mozzarella cheese

16 ounce package of wide egg noodles

1 ½ lb. ground beef

3 ½ package of pepperoni

3 cup(s) of cheddar cheese, grated

Cook the onions and beef in a pan until no longer pink. At the same time, make the noodles in accordance with the directions on the package. Stir the Italian seasoning, mushrooms and spaghetti sauce in with the meat mixture. Drain noodles and set aside. In another separate bowl, mix the two cheeses together. In the slow cooker pour 1/3 of the meat mixture in the bottom, then 1/3 of the noodles, 1/3 of the pepperoni, and then 1/3 of the cheese. Repeat another two times. Cook for 3-4 hours on low until the cheese is melted.

Chapter 5: Tender Chicken

Everyone knows that chicken is the most versatile meat, but combine with a versatile appliance and you have never ending, time efficient and delicious meals!

CHICKEN IN A POT

7-9 hours in a slow cooker
Yields about 6 servings

2 celery ribs, chopped

2 medium onions, diced

½ teaspoon(s) pepper

3 medium carrots, sliced

1 ½ teaspoon(s) salt

3 medium carrots, sliced

1 teaspoon(s) basil

3 lbs. chicken

½ cup(s) of chicken broth

Layer the bottom of the cooker with the vegetables and top with the chicken parts. Mix the final components in a separate bowl and drizzle on top. Cook for 7-9 hours on low.

GOLDEN CHICKEN AND NOODLES

7-8 hours in the slow cooker

Yields about 6 servings

1/8 teaspoon(s) pepper

1 small chopped onion

2-10 ¾ ounce cans of broccoli cheese soup

1 teaspoon(s) basil

6 chicken breast cut in half

2 cup(s) of milk

1 teaspoon(s) salt

Cooked noodles

Mix together the first 6 ingredients. Place chicken parts in the cooker and top with the mixture. For 7-8 hours, cook on the low setting, until chicken juices run clear. Serve over noodles.

ORANGE CHICKEN

4-5 hours in the slow cooker

Yields about 4 servings

3 cup(s) of orange juice

1 cup(s) of green pepper, chopped

1 cup(s) of celery, chopped

3 lb. broiler chicken, cut into parts and skinless

4 ounce can of mushrooms

¼ teaspoon(s) pepper

½ teaspoon(s) salt

4 teaspoon(s) minced onion

1 teaspoon(s) parsley

3 tablespoon(s) cold water

3 tablespoon(s) cornstarch

Cooked Rice

Place the first 9 components into the slow cooker. Cook for at least 4 hours on the low setting. In a different bowl, mix the cornstarch with the water, and then stir into the sauce. After such, cook for another 30-45 minutes. Serve over hot rice.

CHICKEN DINNER

8-9 hours in the slow cooker

Yields about 4 servings

4 carrots, chopped into ½ inch pieces

1/8 teaspoon(s) garlic salt

10 ¾ ounce can of cream of chicken soup

6 red potatoes, chopped

4 chicken breasts

10 ¾ ounce can of cream of mushroom soup

2-4 tablespoon(s) of mashed potato flakes

Put carrots and potatoes into the of the slow cooker and then put in the chicken. In a different dish, mix the garlic salt and soups, then drizzle over the chicken. Cook for about 8-9 hours on low. If you want a thicker the gravy, you can add potato flakes and then cook for an additional 30 min.

CHICKEN A LA KING

8-9 hours in the slow cooker

Yields about 6 servings

3 tablespoon(s) flour

10 ¾ ounce can of cream of chicken soup

Dash of cayenne pepper

¼ teaspoon(s) pepper

½ cup(s) of green pepper, chopped

1 chopped celery rib

1 lb. of chicken breasts

¼ cup(s) of onion, chopped

10 ounce package of peas

2 tablespoon(s) pimentos, diced and drained

Hot cooked rice

Mix the first 4 ingredients into the slow cooker. Add the vegetables and chicken. Next, cook for 7 hours on the low setting and then add the pimentos and peas. Cook for at least 30 more minutes and serve over rice.

ITALIAN CHICKEN

4 hours in the slow cooker
Yields about 4 servings

1 envelope of dry Italian salad dressing
10 ¾ ounce can of cream of chicken soup
¼ cup(s) of water
8 ounce brick of cream cheese
4 ounce can of mushrooms, drained
4 chicken breasts
Hot cooked rice or pasta

Mix salad dressing and water in a small bowl. Put chicken in cooker and drizzle dressing over it. Cook for 3 hours on the low setting. Mix together the rest of the ingredients, except rice or noodles, and place in slow cooker. Stir mixture and continue cooking for an additional hour. Serve over rice or noodles.

APRICOT CHICKEN

4-5 hours in the slow cooker

Yields about 6 servings

2-12 ounce jars of Apricot preserves

6 chicken breasts

1 packet of dry onion soup mix

Hot cooked rice

Mix the soup mix and preserves. Drop chicken into the slow cooker and cover with preserves. Cook for at least 4-5 hours on the low setting and serve over rice.

CHICKEN CACCIATORE

6-8 hours in the slow cooker

Yields about 6 servings

2 onions sliced thin

1 bay leaf

2 minced garlic cloves

¼ teaspoon(s) pepper

8 ounce can of tomato sauce

½ teaspoon(s) basil

4 ounce can of mushrooms

1 teaspoon(s) salt

2 teaspoon(s) oregano

14 ½ ounce can of diced tomatoes

¼ cup(s) of water or dry white wine

3 lb. broiler chicken cut up into parts

Hot cooked pasta

Put the onions into the slow cooker. Top with the remaining components, except for pasta, then cook for about 6-8 hours on the low setting. Discard bay leaf and serve over pasta.

CHICKEN MOLE

6 hours in the slow cooker

Yields about 12 servings

1 teaspoon(s) salt

12 skinless chicken thighs

1 onion chopped

½ cup(s) of toasted sliced onions

2 dried ancho chilies, no stems or seeds

¼ cup(s) of raisins

3 tablespoon(s) olive oil

3 ounce chopped bittersweet chocolate

3 garlic cloves

28 ounce can of whole tomatoes, drained

1 chipotle pepper in adobo sauce

½ teaspoon(s) cinnamon

¾ teaspoon(s) cumin

Fresh cilantro

Put chicken into slow cooker and sprinkle with salt. Pu the rest of the components, except the cilantro, in a food processor and mix. Drizzle over chicken and cook for at least 6-8 hours on the low setting. Serve chicken with a pinch of cilantro.

CHICKEN MARINARA

4 hours in the slow cooker

Yields about 4 servings

1 minced garlic clove

1 chopped tomato

2 cup(s) of marinara sauce

1 ½ teaspoon(s) Italian seasoning

½ cup(s) of Italian salad dressing

4 chicken breasts

Hot cooked pasta

Shredded mozzarella cheese

Mix together the first 5 ingredients. Put chicken into slow cooker and cover with sauce. Cooke for 4 hours on low. Serve over pasta and sprinkle with cheese.

HONEY PINEAPPLE CHICKEN

3-4 hours in the slow cooker
Yields about 12 servings

8 ounce can of unsweetened crushed pineapple with the liquid
½ cup(s) of honey
2 tablespoon(s) soy sauce
1 cup(s) of brown sugar, packed
2 tablespoon(s) mustard
¼ cup(s) of melted butter
1/3 cup(s) of lemon juice
3 lbs. chicken breasts, skinless and boneless
2 tablespoon(s) canola oil

Brown chicken in a pan with the oil on both sides and place into the cooker. Next, mix together the last of the components and drizzle on chicken. Then, cook for 3-4 hours on low. Serve with pineapple chunks.

CHICKEN AFRITAD

7-8 hours in the slow cooker
Yields about 6 servings

½ cup(s) of soy sauce
½ cup(s) of olive oil
1 lb. chicken breasts, cubed
1 lemon juiced
Dash of pepper to taste
1 sliced green bell pepper
3 minced garlic cloves
1 cup(s) of green peas
1 sliced red bell pepper
3 cubed red potatoes
1 sliced yellow bell pepper
2 chopped carrots
1 sliced onion
2 cubed tomatoes

Put the first 5 ingredients into the slow cooker and let marinate for 10-15 minutes. Meanwhile mix the rest of the components together and pour into cooker after the chicken is done marinating. Cook for 7-8 hours on low.

Chapter 6: Flavorful Pork

Pork is one of those meats that is so flavorful. It can be paired with sweet fruits and preserves or mixed into a salty dish that is sure to please!

MUSHROOM PORK TENDERLOIN

4-5 hours in the slow cooker
Yields about 6 servings

10 ¾ ounce can of French onion soup
10 ¾ ounce can of golden mushroom soup
2-1 lb. pork tenderloins
10 ¾ ounce can of cream of mushroom soup

Mix together the soups in a bowl. Put tenderloin into the slow cooker then cover with soup. Cook for at least 4-5 hours on the low setting. Serve over rice or mashed potatoes.

SWEET AND SOUR RIBS

8-10 hours in the slow cooker

Yields about 8 servings

20 ounce can of pineapple tidbits, with liquid

½ cup(s) of of green pepper, thinly sliced

½ cup(s) of of onion, thinly sliced

¼ cup(s) of tomato paste

¼ cup(s) of cider vinegar

½ cup(s) of brown sugar, packed

2-8 ounce cans of tomato sauce

1 minced garlic clove

2 tablespoon(s) Worcestershire sauce

4 lbs. country style pork ribs, boneless

Salt and Pepper

Combine the top 9 ingredients into a bowl. Put ribs into the cooker then drizzle with the mixture. Cook for 8-10 hours on low. Thicken sauce if you desire and use salt and pepper to improve the taste if desired.

POLISH KRAUT AND APPLES

4-5 hours in the slow cooker

Yields about 4 servings

1 lb. of cooked Kielbasa or Polish sausage, chopped up

14 ounce jar of sauerkraut, drained and washed

3 medium tart apples, peeled then cut into wedges

¾ cup(s) of apple juice

½ teaspoon(s) caraway seed

1/8 teaspoon(s) pepper

½ cup(s) of brown sugar, packed

Put half of the sauerkraut into the slow cooker. Then put the apples and sausage and cap with remaining ingredient/sauerkraut. Cook for about 4-5 hours on low.

HAM AND HASH BROWNS

7-8 hours in the slow cooker

Yields about 4 servings

2 ounce jar of drained pimentos

2 cup(s) of of fully cooked ham, cubed

28 ounce bag of hash browns

10 ¾ ounce can of cheddar cheese soup

¼ teaspoon(s) pepper

¾ cup(s) of milk

Find a bowl and join the soup, pepper, and milk in it. Stir the pimentos, ham, and hash browns into the slow cooker. Mix in the soup and for 7-8 hours, cook on low then serve.

TENDER PORK ROAST

8-9 hours in the slow cooker

Yields about 8 servings

¾ cup(s) of soy sauce

8 ounce can of tomato sauce

½ cup(s) of sugar

2 teaspoon(s) ground mustard

3 lb. boneless pork roast

Get a bowl and combine the first 4 ingredients in it. Cut the roast in half and drop into the slow cooker. Top with the sauce and cook for about 8-9 hours on low.

PARMESAN PORK ROAST

5-6 hours in the slow cooker

Yields about 10 servings

½ teaspoon(s) salt

½ cup(s) of honey

2 tablespoon(s) olive oil

2 tablespoon(s) basil

2 tablespoon(s) minced garlic

3 tablespoon(s) soy sauce

4 lb. pork loin roast

2/3 cup(s) of grated parmesan cheese

2 tablespoon(s) cornstarch

¼ cup(s) of cold water

Get a bowl and combine the first seven ingredients in it. Afterwards, slice the pork in half and place in the cooker. Drizzle the sauce into the cooker and for at least 5-6 hours, cook on low. Remove roast and transfer liquid to a sauce pan. Mix the cornstarch with the water in a small bowl while bringing the pork sauce to a boil. Then stir in cornstarch and wait until it boils again and cook for another 2 minutes until it thickens. Slice roast and drizzle with gravy.

SLOW COOKER CHOPS

4-5 hours in the slow cooker

Yields about 10 servings

10 trimmed boneless pork chops

10 ¾ ounce can of cream of onion soup

1 large sliced onion

1 ounce packet of onion soup mix

1 ounce packet of ranch dressing mix

5 fluid ounce water

10 ¾ ounce can of cream of mushroom soup

Salt and Pepper

Put 1/3 of the onions in the slow cooker, then 5 of the chops. Repeat once more and then place remaining onions on top. Mix the rest of the components into a bowl and pour over the top. Cook for at least 4-5 hours on low and serve.

Chapter 7: Bonus! Desserts

What would life be without dessert? More importantly, what would a well-rounded cookbook be without the ability to help you make that dessert?

PUMPKIN PIE PUDDING

6-7 hours in the slow cooker

Yields about 6-7 servings

½ cup(s) of biscuit/baking mix

12 ounce can of evaporated milk

2 tablespoon(s) melted butter

15 ounce can of solid-pack pumpkin

2 beaten eggs

2 teaspoon(s) vanilla

2 ½ teaspoon(s) pumpkin pie spice

¾ cup(s) of sugar

Ice cream or whipped topping

Pour all the ingredients into a bowl, except the ice cream or whipped topping, and mix together. Spray the slow cooker with a nonstick spray and transfer pudding into cooker. Cook for 6-7 on low.

MINISTER'S DELIGHT

2-3 hours in the slow cooker

Yields about 10-12 servings

18 ¼ ounce box of cake mix

½ cup(s) of melted butter

21 ounce can of cherry or apple pie filling

1/3 cup(s) of chopped walnuts

In a bowl mix together butter and cake mix. Pour pie filling into slow cooker and cover with crumbly cake mix. Top with walnuts. Cook for 2-3 hours on low.

APPLE DELIGHT

3 hours in the slow cooker
Yields about 4-6 servings

¼ cup(s) of old fashioned oats
8 peeled and cored apples, sliced
¾ melted butter
2 tablespoon(s) lemon juice
¼ teaspoon(s) ground cinnamon
½ to 1 cup(s) of chopped pecans
1/3 cup(s) of sugar

Mix everything together in a slow cooker then for 3 hours, cook on the high setting. Stir occasionally.

CHOCOLATE PUDDING CAKE

6-7 hours in the slow cooker
Yields about 10-12 servings

3.9 box of chocolate pudding mix

¾ cup(s) of vegetable oil

4 eggs

1 cup(s) of water

2 cup(s) of sour cream

1 cup(s) of semisweet chocolate chips

18 ¼ ounce box of chocolate cake mix

Ice cream

Mix the top 6 components in a bowl for 2 minutes. Mix in the chocolate chips and coat slow cooker with a nonstick spray. Dump mixture into cooker and cook for between 6-7 hours on the low setting. Insert a toothpick into the middle of the cake; it's done when it comes out with moist crumbs. Serve warm with ice cream.

SWEET BREAD PUDDING

3 hours in the slow cooker

Yields about 6 servings

2 cup(s) of milk

¼ cup(s) of melted butter

¼ cup(s) of sugar

4 eggs

½ teaspoon(s) vanilla

¼ teaspoon(s) ground nutmeg

8 cup(s) of cubed old bread (white, wheat, Hawaiian, potato, cinnamon rolls, etc.)

1 cup(s) of raisins

Get a bowl and mix the first six ingredients in it. Put bread into the slow cooker and drizzle milk mixture on top. Top with raisins and cook for 3 hours on low.

SPICED APRICOT CIDER

2 hours in the slow cooker

Yields about 6 servings.

2-3-inch cinnamon sticks

2 whole cloves

2 cup(s) of water

¼ cup(s) of sugar

¼ cup(s) of lemon juice

2-12 ounce cans od apricot nectar

Combine all the components and for 2 hours, cook on low. Remove cloves and cinnamon sticks to serve. Replace a cinnamon stick into each cup(s) of if you want.

PART III

Chapter 1: Mastering the Air Fryer

How to Use the Air Fryer

The Air Fryer provides you with a way to eat healthier by providing you healthier ways

to prepare your recipes without losing the texture and flavor of your homemade meals and snacks. From *French toast sticks* to *air fried ravioli* or that plateful of *Mozzarella sticks* you have been craving; you will enjoy every morsel as you learn how to prepare the recipes provided in this book.

Useful Guidelines for Recipe Measurement

With so many recipes in circulation for the air fryer (AF) provided greatly due to the Internet; you may begin to notice the many different ways they are written. This is because they travel worldwide and the best ones become viral.

These are some of the conversion tables that will guide you through the process:

> *Celsius to Fahrenheit*
>
> *Grams to Cups*
>
> *Grams to Pounds*
>
> *Milliliters to Cups*

Other abbreviations can include the following:

- Cup = C.
- Tablespoon = Tbsp. = T.
- Teaspoon = tsp. = t.

Going by the 'rule-of-thumb,' a handful should be between 1/3 cup to ½ cup (more or less). You might also hear a smidge or a pinch which is usually ¼ teaspoon or a dollop is usually a heaping tablespoon.

Tips for Using the Air Fryer

Tip #1: Many pre-made packaged food items you already purchase can be cooked using the Air Fryer. Each food may vary with its cooking time. As a guideline, reduce the cooking times by about 70% compared to times in a conventional oven.

Tip #2: While cooking smaller items such as fries or wings; you can make sure they are cooking evenly by shaking the basket several times during the cooking process.

Tip #3: It is important to pat food items dry if you have marinated or soaked them in to help eliminate splattering or excessive smoke.

Tip #4: It is tempting when you are in a rush to attempt to overload the Air fryer. Don't put too much in the cooking basket at one time. You won't receive the best results if the air cannot make the 360° turns that make the cooker so unique.

Tip #5: Allow at least three minutes warm-up time each time you use the fryer so it can reach its correct starting temperature.

Tip #6: When it comes time to clean the cooking basket, loosen any food particles remaining attached to the basket. Soak each of the attachments in a soapy water solution before scrubbing or placing it in the dishwasher.

Tip #7: If you use aluminum foil or parchment paper, leave a one-half-inch space around the bottom edge of the basket.

Tip #8: Cooking sprays are an excellent choice to spray on your food before cooking. You can also spray the mesh of the cooking basket to keep anything from sticking to its surface.

Proof You Should Own an Air Fryer

Benefit #1: It is a beginner's treat. You can locate your favorite recipes and whip up a remarkable meal at home in half of the time. The machine does the hard work for you. All you need to do is program the temperature and times.

Benefit #2: The Fryer Needs Less Oil. It won't be necessary to add oil to the cooker if you have frozen products which are meant for baking. You only need to adjust the timer and cook. All of the excess fat will drip away into a tray beneath the basket.

You can cook whatever meats you enjoy and receive delicious and healthy results. You will understand this once you begin trying out some of these new recipes.

For example; you can cook French fries with a tablespoon of oil versus a vat of oil.

Benefit #3: No Oily Clean Up: You only need to remove the cooking bowl, drip pan, or the cooking basket. It is inside a cover which means you won't have oil vapor deposits on the walls, floors, or countertops.

You can use the dishwasher to clean the movable parts. You can also use a sponge to clean the bits of food that might be stuck to the AF surfaces.

Benefit #4: Purchase Less Oil: It is possible to splurge on the more expensive oils since you only use such a minimal amount.

Benefit #5: Multitasking Features: The Air Fryer is capable of functioning as so many products, whether you need an oven, a hot grill, a toaster, a skillet, or a deep fryer—it is your answer! It can be used for breakfast, lunch, dinner, desserts, and even snacks.

Benefit #6: Safety Functions: The machine will automatically shut down when the cooking time is completed. You will have less burned or overheated food items.

The unit will not slip because of the non-slip feet which help eliminate the risk of the machine from falling off of the countertop. The closed cooking system helps prevent burns from hot oil or other foods.

Now that you know how to avoid some of the pitfalls you may have with your new Air Fryer unit; you can begin planning which delicious treat you want to test first!

Chapter 2: Air Fryer Breakfast Recipes

Apple Dumplings

Ingredients

2 Tbsp. raisins

2 small apples (peeled—cored)

1 Tbsp. brown sugar

2 sheets puff pastry

2 Tbsp. melted butter

Instructions

1) Preheat the Air Fryer to 356°F.

2) Mix the sugar and raisins.

3) Place each apple on one of the pastry sheets and fill with the raisins/sugar.

4) Fold the pastry over until the apple and raisins are fully covered.

5) Place them on a piece of foil so they cannot fall through the fryer.

6) Thoroughly brush them with the melted butter.

7) Set the timer for 25 minutes. It is ready when the apples are sold and browned.

Note: Be sure to use very small apples for this yummy treat.

Banana Fritters

Ingredients

8 ripe peeled bananas

3 Tbsp. corn flour

One egg white

3 Tbsp. vegetable oil

¾ cup breadcrumbs

Instructions

1) Preheat the fryer at 356°F.

2) In a skillet using the low heat setting; pour the oil and toss in the breadcrumbs, cooking until golden brown.

3) Use the flour to coat the bananas; dip them into the egg white, and coat them with the bread crumbs.

4) Place the bananas on a single layer of the basket and air fry for eight minutes.

5) Remove and sit on paper towels.

What a delicious treat to be served warm!

Tip: If you have too many breadcrumbs; you can place them in the fridge in an airtight container to use sometime in the future.

French Toast Sticks

Ingredients

2 gently beaten eggs

4 slices of desired bread

2 tablespoons soft margarine or butter

Cinnamon

Salt

Ground cloves

Nutmeg

Garnish: Maple syrup

Instructions

1) Preheat the Air Fryer to 356°F.

2) Whisk the eggs, a shake of nutmeg, cloves, and cinnamon together in a small bowl.

3) Spread butter on both sides of the bread, and cut them into strips.

4) Dredge each of the cuts in the egg mix, and arrange in the fryer. (You will need to make two batches.)

5) Pause the fryer after two minutes, remove the pan, and spray the bread with cooking spray.

6) Flip and spray the other side, returning them to the AF for an additional four minutes, making sure they do not burn.

7) It's ready when it is golden brown; serve them immediately.

Garnish with some maple syrup or whipped cream.

Yields: Two Servings

Bacon and Eggs

Ingredients

4 eggs

12 (1/2-inch thick) slices of bacon

Pepper and salt

1 Tablespoon butter

2 sliced croissants

4 Tablespoons softened butter

BBQ Sauce Ingredients

1 C. ketchup

¼ C. apple cider vinegar

2 Tablespoons each:

- Brown sugar

- Molasses

½ teaspoon each:

- Onion powder

- Mustard powder

1 Tablespoon Worcestershire sauce

½ teaspoon liquid smoke

Instructions

1) Preset the temperature in the Air Fryer to 390°F.

2) On the stovetop, using medium heat—mix the molasses, ketchup, brown sugar, vinegar, onion powder, and mustard power using a small saucepot. Whisk the liquid smoke and Worcestershire sauce into the mixture to blend thoroughly. Cook until the sauce thickens. Add additional flavoring as desired.

3) Place the bacon on the trays and cook for five minutes. Remove and brush the bacon with the barbecue sauce –flip—and brush the other side—return to the cooker and continue cooking another five minutes.

4) Butter the halved croissant and toast it in the fryer.

5) In the meantime, use a non-stick pan using the med-low setting on the stovetop—melt the butter. Add four eggs to the pan, cooking until the white starts setting—flip and cook about thirty more seconds.

6) Remove from the pan, and enjoy with the bacon and croissant.

Yields: Four Servings

Cheesy Mushroom, Ham, and Egg

Ingredients

3 slices honey shaved ham

1 croissant

4 halved cherry tomatoes

4 small quartered button mushrooms

1 egg

1.8 ounces mozzarella or cheddar cheese

Optional: ½ roughly chopped rosemary sprig

Instructions

1) Lightly grease a baking dish with butter to prevent the mixture from sticking.

2) Preset the Air Fryer to 320°F.

3) Place the ingredients on 2 layers with cheese in the center and top layer.

4) Make a space in the center of the ham and crack the egg.

5) Sprinkle the rosemary and a smidgen of salt and pepper for flavoring over the mixture.

6) Put it into the preheated basket for eight minutes. Take the croissant out of the AF after four minutes to allow more time for the egg to cook.

Yields: One Serving

Scrambled Eggs

Ingredients

2 eggs

Pepper and salt to taste

Instructions

1) Preset the Air Fryer to 284°F for about five minutes.

2) Put the butter in the fryer to melt, and spread it out evenly.

3) Empty the eggs and any other ingredients such as cheese or tomatoes.

4) Open the AF every few minutes to whisk to the desired yellow and fluffy consistency.

Make a scrambled egg sandwich or with toast on the side.

Air Fryer Spinach Frittata

For a fantastic meal good for breakfast, lunch, dinnertime, or anytime; you have found it!

Ingredients

1/3 package (or so) of spinach

1 small minced red onion

Mozzarella cheese

3 eggs

Instructions

1) Preset the Air Fryer at 356°F for at least three minutes.

2) Add oil to a baking pan for one minute.

3) Add the onions and continue cooking for two to three minutes; toss in the spinach and cook three to five minutes additional minutes.

4) Whisk in the eggs, add the seasonings, cheese, and add to the pan.

5) Cook for eight minutes. Season with salt and pepper.

Bacon Wrapped Tater Tots

Ingredients

3 tablespoons sour cream

1 pound sliced bacon (medium)

1 large bag crispy tater tots

4 scallions

½ cup shredded cheddar cheese

Instructions

1) Preheat the Air Fryer to 400°F.

2) Wrap each of the tots in bacon and place them into the fryer basket. Don't overcrowd, keep them in a single layer.

3) Set the AF timer for 8 minutes.

4) When the timer beeps; place the tots on a plate.

5) Serve with the scallions and cheese garnish. Add a dash of sour cream and enjoy.

Yields: Four Servings

Buttermilk Biscuits

These have to be considered for breakfast also because they are so delicious!

Ingredients

½ C. cake flour

¾ tsp. salt

1-¼ C. all-purpose flour

¼ tsp. baking soda

1 teaspoon granulated sugar

½ tsp. baking powder

¾ C. buttermilk

4 Tbsp. unsalted cold butter (cut into cubes) + melt 1 Tbsp.

Optional for Serving:

Honey or preserves

Butter

Note: Additional flour is needed for dusting the counter or cutting board.

Instructions

1) Preheat the Air Fryer to 400°F.

1) Sift together the all-purpose flour, sugar, cake flour, baking soda, and the salt in a medium mixing dish.

2) Use a pastry cutter (or your fingers) to blend the ingredients into pea-sized consistency. Pour in the buttermilk and stir using a rubber spatula (or your hands), and make a dough ball. Try not to over-mix the dough.

3) Sprinkle some flour on the counter surface and begin to press the dough into about a ½-inch thickness. It should be approximately eight inches in diameter.

4) Use a cutter to cut the dough into biscuits; dip the tip of the tip of the cutter with the flour making a swift cut. If you twist the dough; it could prevent it from rising.

5) Place the biscuits in a pan and brush them with the melted butter. Place the dough in the basket of the fryer and set the timer for eight minutes.

Enjoy the finished product with some honey or your favorite preserves, jam, or jelly.

Vegan Mini Bacon Wrapped Burritos

Ingredients

2 servings Tofu Scramble or Vegan Egg

2-3 tablespoons tamari

2 tablespoons cashew butter

1-2 tablespoons water

1-2 tablespoons liquid smoke

4 pieces of rice paper

Vegetable Add-Ins

8 strips roasted red pepper

1/3 cup sweet potato roasted cubes

1 small sautéed tree broccoli

Handful of greens (kale, spinach, etc.)

6-8 stalks of fresh asparagus

Instructions

1) Line the pan used for baking with parchment. Preheat the Air Fryer to 350°F.

2) Whisk the tamari, cashew butter, water, and liquid smoke; set to the side.

3) Prepare the fillings.

4) Hold a rice paper under cool running water—getting both sides wet—just a second. Place on the plate to fill.

5) Start by filling the ingredients –just-off- from the center—leaving the sides of the paper free.

6) Fold in two of the sides as you would when you make a burrito. Seal them and dip each one in the liquid smoke mixture—coating completely.

7) Cook until crispy; usually about eight to ten minutes.

Yields: Four Mini Burritos

Chapter 3: Lunch Recipes

Grilled Cheese Sandwich

Ingredients

½ Cup sharp cheddar cheese

4 Slices white bread or brioche

¼ Cup melted butter

Instructions

1) Pre-set the Air Fryer temperature to 360°F.

2) Spread butter on each side of all of the bread slices, and put the cheese on two of them; putting them together. Cook until browned, about five to seven minutes.

Yields: Serves Two

Cheeseburger Mini Sliders

Ingredients

6 Slices cheddar cheese

1 Pound ground beef

6 Dinner Rolls

Black pepper and Salt

Instructions

1) Pre-set the heat on the Air Fryer to 390°F.

2) Form 6 (2 ½-ounce) patties and flavor with the pepper and salt

3) Place the burgers on the AF basket for ten minutes.

4) Take them from the cooker and add the cheese; returning to the Air Fryer for an additional minute until the cheese melts. Yummy!

Yields: Serves Three

Pigs In A Blanket

Ingredients

1 (Eight-ounce) Can crescent rolls

1 (Twelve-ounce) Package cocktail franks

Instructions

1) Preheat the Air Fryer to 330°F.

2) Drain the franks and thoroughly dry them using two paper towels.

3) Slice the dough into strips of about 1 ½ inches x 1-inch (rectangular).

4) Roll the dough around the franks leaving the ends open. Put them in the freezer to firm-up for about five minutes.

5) Take them out, and put them in the AF for six to eight minutes. Adjust the temperature to 390°F, and continue to cook for approximately three minutes.

Yields: Serves Four

Chicken

AF Chicken 'Fried'

Ingredients

2 chicken thighs (skinless)

3 sprigs fresh parsley

Garlic powder (to dust the thighs)

Salt and black pepper if desired

½ a lemon

Chili flakes as you like

1 to 2 sprigs fresh rosemary

Instructions

1) Rinse the thighs. Drain them between two paper towels. (Discard the towels and wash your hands.)

2) Clean the rosemary sprigs and remove the stems. Chop or mince the parsley.

3) *For the Marinate*: Combine the salt and pepper, garlic powder, rosemary leaves, parsley, chili flakes, and lemon juice. Add the thighs and marinate overnight in the refrigerator.

4) *Preheat the Air Fryer*: Set the AF to 356°F.

5) Grill for 12 minutes.

Note: Times may vary depending on the thickness/size of the thighs.

AF Buffalo Chicken Wings

Ingredients

5 chicken wings (about 14 ounces)

½ teaspoon garlic powder (optional)

2 teaspoons cayenne pepper

2 tablespoons red hot sauce

1 tablespoon (15 grams) melted butter

Fresh black pepper and salt to taste

Instructions

1) Preheat the Air Fryer at 356°F.

2) Cut the wings into three sections (the end tip, mid joint, and drumstick). Pat each one thoroughly dry using a paper towel. Wash your wash right away to prevent cross contamination.

3) Combine a dash of pepper and salt, the garlic powder, and cayenne pepper in a plate. Lightly coat the wings with the powder.

4) Place the chicken on the wire rack and back for 15 minutes; turning once at 7 minutes.

5) Combine the hot sauce, and melted butter in a dish to garnish the baked chicken when it is time to be served.

Notes: Save and freeze the end tip for preparing chicken stock.

You can increase the cayenne pepper if you want it hotter.

Country Style Chicken Tenders

Ingredients

¾ pounds chicken tenders

2 tablespoons olive oil

½ teaspoon salt

2 beaten eggs

½ cup all-purpose flour

½ cup seasoned breadcrumbs

1 teaspoon black pepper

Instructions

1) Preheat the Air Fryer heat to 330°F.

2) Set up three separate dishes for the flour, eggs, and breadcrumbs.

3) Blend the salt, pepper and bread crumbs. Pour in the oil with the breadcrumbs and mix. Put the chicken tenders into the flour, and the eggs. Coat evenly with the breadcrumbs. Shake the excess off before placing in the Air Fryer basket.

4) Cook for ten minutes at 330°F and increase to 390°F for five minutes or until they are a nice golden brown.

Chinese Chicken Wings

Ingredients

4 chicken wings

Salt and pepper to taste

1 tablespoon each:

- Chinese spice

- Mixed spice

- Soy sauce

Instructions

Preheat the AF to 180°C/356°F.

1) Add the seasonings into a large mixing container—stirring thoroughly.

2) Blend the seasonings over the chicken wings until each piece is covered.

3) Put some aluminum foil on the base of the AF (similar to how you cover a baking tray), and add the chicken sprinkling any remnants over the chicken. Cook for 15 minutes.

4) Flip the chicken and cook another 15 minutes at 200C/392F.

Yields: Two Servings

Chicken Pot Pie

Ingredients

6 chicken tenders

2 potatoes

1 ½ cups condensed cream of celery soup

¾ cup heavy cream

1 thyme sprig

1 whole dried bay leaf

5 refrigerated buttermilk biscuits (dough)

1 tablespoon milk

1 egg yolk

Instructions

1) Preheat the Air Fryer at 320°F.

2) Peel and dice the potatoes.

3) Mix all of the ingredients in a pan except for the milk, egg yolk, and biscuits. Bring them to a boil using medium heat.

4) Empty the mixture into the baking tin and use some aluminum foil to cover the top. Place the pan into the fry basket. Set the timer for 15 minutes.

5) Meanwhile, after the pie completes the cycle make an egg wash with the milk and egg yolk. Place the biscuits on the baking pan and brush with the egg wash mixture.

6) Set the timer to 300°F for an additional ten minutes.

7) Your pie is ready when the biscuits are golden brown.

Yields: Four Servings

Tarragon Chicken

Ingredients

1 skinless and boneless chicken breast

⅛ Teaspoon fresh ground black pepper

½ Teaspoon unsalted butter

⅛ Teaspoon kosher salt

¼ Cup dried tarragon

Instructions

1) Pre-set the cooker to 390°F.

2) Cut a piece of heavy-duty aluminum foil—approximately 12 x 12 or you can double a regular strength one and fold in half. Put the chicken on it.

3) Place the butter and tarragon on top of the chicken and flavor with pepper and salt—loosely wrapping the chicken for minimal airflow.

4) Cook for 12 minutes in the Air Fryer basket, remove the meal from the wrapper and enjoy.

Beef

Beef Roll Ups

Ingredients

6 slices provolone cheese

2 pounds beef flank steak

3 tablespoons pesto

¾ cup fresh baby spinach

1 teaspoon each sea salt and ground black pepper

3-ounces roasted red bell peppers

Instructions

1) Preheat the Air Fryer cooker to 400°F.

2) Open the steak up and add the butter and pesto evenly on the meat.

3) Layer in the spinach, peppers, and cheese about three-quarters the way down through the meat.

4) Roll the mixture and secure it with toothpicks or skewers.

5) Set the timer for 14 minutes; flipping the beef halfway through the cooking process.

6) Let the meat rest for a minimum of ten minutes before attempting to cut and serve the tasty delight.

Yields: Four Servings

Air Fried Ravioli

Ingredients

1 package meat or cheese ravioli

1 jar Marinara sauce

2 C. breadcrumbs (Italian-style)

1 C. buttermilk

¼ C. Parmesan cheese

Olive oil

Note: Purchase the sauce and ravioli ready-made.

Instructions

1) Preheat the Air Fryer to 200°F.

2) Empty the buttermilk into a container and dip the ravioli.

3) Put a spoonful of oil to the breadcrumbs. Coat the ravioli with the crumbs.

4) Add the ravioli into the AF on baking paper for around five minutes.

Roasted Veggie Pasta Salad

Ingredients

4 ounces brown mushrooms

1 red onion

1 yellow squash

1 zucchini

1 each bell peppers

- Red

- Green

- Orange

Pinch of Fresh ground pepper and salt

1 teaspoon Italian seasoning

1 cup grape tomatoes

½ cup pitted Kalamata olives

1 pound cooked Rigatoni or Penne Rigate

¼ cup olive oil

2 tablespoons fresh chopped basil

3 tablespoons balsamic vinegar

Instructions

1) Cut the squash and zucchini into half-moons. Cut the peppers into large chunks and slice the red onion. Slice the tomatoes and olives in half.

2) Preheat the Air Fryer to 380°F.

3) Put the mushrooms, peppers, red onion, squash, and zucchini in a large container.

4) Drizzle with some of the oil—tossing well. Sprinkle in the pepper, salt, and Italian seasoning.

5) Place in the Air Fryer until the veggies are soft (not mushy), usually about for 12 to 15 minutes. For even roasting; shake the basket about halfway through the cooking cycle.

6) Combine the roasted veggies, olives, cooked pasta, and tomatoes, in a large container; mix well. Add the vinegar, and toss. (Use as little oil as possible, just enough to coat the vegetables.)

7) Keep it refrigerated until ready to serve—adding the fresh basil for last.

Yields: Six to Eight Servings

Chapter 4: Air Fryer Dinner Recipes

Chicken and Turkey Recipes

Lemon Rosemary Chicken

Ingredients

1 pound chicken (350 g)

For the Marinate:

1 tablespoon soy sauce

½ tablespoon olive oil

1 teaspoon minced ginger

For the Sauce:

3 tablespoons brown sugar

1 tablespoon oyster sauce

½ wedge-cut lemon in skins

Optional: 15 g (0.5 ounces) fresh rosemary

Instructions

1) Leave the skin on the rosemary and chop.

2) Blend all of the marinade components. Pour over the chicken. Let them cool off in the fridge for about thirty minutes.

3) Place the marinade and chicken in a baking dish, and bake for six minutes in the AF at 392°F.

4) Blend all of the sauce ingredients (minus the lemon).

5) Pour the mixture over the chicken when it is about half baked.

6) Place the lemon wedges in the pan evenly and squeeze so the zest will heighten the flavor of the chicken. Continue baking for an additional 13 minutes turning to ensure all of the pieces are browned evenly.

Note: You can omit the rosemary.

Jamaican Chicken Meatballs

Ingredients

1 large peeled and diced onion

2 large chicken breasts

1 teaspoon chili powder

2 tablespoons honey

Pepper and salt to taste

3 tablespoons soy sauce

1 tablespoon each:

- Dry mustard

- Cumin

- Thyme

- Basil

Optional: 2 teaspoons Jerk Paste

Instructions

1) Using a blender—mince the chicken; add the onion and mince; mix well. Toss in the Jamaican seasonings and blend again. Make ten medium balls.

2) Place on the baking mat in the AF and cook at 356°F or 180°C.

3) Put them on a stick when done cooking and some use of the extra sauce over the meatballs.

4) Add several herbs on the top, serve, and enjoy.

Yields: Ten Servings

Note: In case you are not aware; jerk paste is a combination of brown spices, ginger, peppers, and thyme.

Roast Turkey Breast

Ingredients

1 tablespoon ground black pepper

8 pounds bone-in turkey breast

2 tablespoon each:

- Olive oil

- Sea salt

Instructions

1) Preheat the Air Fryer on 360°F.

2) Rub the turkey with olive oil and flavor with the seasonings.

3) Put the turkey in the preheated basket for 20 minutes.

4) When done, flip it over and adjust the cooking time for another 20 minutes (also at 360°F).

5) The breast of turkey is done when it registers 165°F when thermometer tested.

6) Allow the meat rest a minimum of 20 minutes before serving.

Spicy Rolled Meat

Ingredients

1 (1.6 pounds/500 g) turkey breast fillet

½ tsp. chili powder

1 ½ tsp. ground cumin

1 crushed garlic clove

1 tsp. cinnamon

2 Tbsp. olive oil

1 small finely chopped onion

2 Tbsp. flat-leafed parsley (finely chopped)

Needed: Rolled meat String

Instructions

1) Preset the heat on the Air Fryer at 356°F/180°C.

2) Put the meat onto a cutting board with the short end facing you. Cut the full length of the fillet. Stop cutting about (2 cm, 13/16inches) from the edge and about 1/3 of the way from the top. Fold this section open and cut it again from this side and open the meat.

3) Combine the cinnamon, chili powder, 1 teaspoon of salt, pepper, and cumin in a mixing container in a small mixing container. Pour in the oil.

4) Spoon one tablespoon of the mixture into a small dish and add the parsley and onion.

5) Use the mixture to coat the meat.

6) Tie it starting at 1 ¼-inch intervals.

7) Rub the outside with the herbal mixture for about 40 minutes or until nicely browned.

Yields: Four Servings

Fish and Seafood

Salmon Patties

Ingredients

1 salmon portion (about 7 ounces)

3 large russet potatoes (about 14 ounces)

1/3 cup frozen veggies (parboiled & drained)

2 dill sprinkles

Dash of salt and pepper

1 egg

Coating: breadcrumbs

Olive oil spray

Instructions

1) Set the Air Fryer to 356°F.

2) Peel and chop the potatoes into small bits and boil for about ten minutes.

3) Mash and place in the fridge to chill.

4) Grill the salmon for five minutes, flake it apart and set it to the side.

5) Combine all of the ingredients and shape into patties.

6) Evenly coat with the breadcrumbs, and spray them with a bit of olive spray.

7) Place in the Air Fryer for ten to twelve minutes.

Yields: Six to Eight Patties

Dill Salmon

Ingredients for the Salmon

4 (6-ounce pieces) or 1 ½ pounds salmon

1 Pinch of salt

2 Teaspoons olive oil

Ingredients for the Dill Sauce

½ cup each:

- Sour cream

- Non-fat Greek yogurt

- 2 (finely chopped) tablespoons dill

- 1 Pinch of salt

Instructions

1) Preheat the AF to 270°F.

2) Slice the salmon into the four portions, and drizzle with half of the oil (1 teaspoon). Flavor with a pinch of salt and add to the basket for about 20 to 23 minutes.

3) *Make the Sauce*: Blend the sour cream, yogurt, salt, and dill in a mixing container. Pour the sauce over the cooked salmon as a garnish with a pinch of the chopped dill.

Yields: Serves Four

Halibut Steak With a Teriyaki Glazed Sauce

Ingredients

1 Lb. halibut steak

Ingredients for the Marinade

½ cup mirin (Japanese cooking wine)

2/3 cup low-sodium soy sauce

¼ cup sugar

¼ cup orange juice

2 tablespoons lime juice

¼ teaspoon each:

- Ground ginger

- Crushed red pepper flakes

1 smashed garlic clove

Instructions

1) Preheat the Air Fryer to 390°F.

2) Combine all of the marinade ingredients in a saucepan, bring it to a boil and reduce to medium heat; cool.

3) Pour half of the marinade in a resealable plastic bag with the halibut. Chill in the fridge for thirty minutes.

4) Cook the halibut for ten to twelve minutes. Brush some of the remaining glaze over the steak.

5) Serve over top a bed of rice. Add a little basil or mint for some extra jazz.

Yields: Serves Three

Cajun Shrimp

Ingredients

1 tablespoon olive oil

½ teaspoon Old Bay seasoning

16 to 20 (1 ¼ pounds) tiger shrimp

¼ teaspoon each:

- smoked paprika

- cayenne pepper

1 pinch of salt

1) Preheat the Air Fryer to 390°F.

2) Mix all of the ingredients and coat the shrimp with the oil and spices.

3) Place the shrimp into the basket and cook for five minutes.

4) Complement the meal with some rice and place the shrimp on top for a tasty luncheon treat.

Coconut Shrimp

Ingredients

12 Large raw shrimp

1 tablespoon cornstarch

½ tablespoon oil

1 Cup each:

- Raw egg whites

- Unsweetened dried coconut

- White all-purpose flour

- Panko

Instructions

1) Drain the shrimp on towels

2) Preheat the AF to 350°F.

3) Combine the coconut and panko in a container and set it to the side; blend the cornstarch and oil in another dish.

4) Put the egg whites into another container, and a third one for the coconut mix.

5) Cover each shrimp in the cornstarch mix, the egg whites, and lastly the coconut mixture.

6) Cook for ten minutes; flipping them after five minutes for even cooking.

Yields: Three Servings

Beef

Rib Steak

Ingredients

1 Tablespoon of steak rub

2 pounds rib steaks

1 Tablespoon of olive oil

Instructions

1) Before it is time to cook; preheat the Air Fryer to 400°F.

2) Flavor the meat on all areas with the oil and rub.

3) Put it in the basket for 14 minutes, flipping after seven minutes.

4) Let it rest for at least ten minutes before you slice and serve.

Yields: Two Servings

Stromboli

Ingredients

1 (12-ounce) refrigerated pizza crust

¾ cup Mozzarella shredded cheese

3 cups shredded cheddar cheese

1 tablespoon milk

1 egg yolk

1/3 pound sliced cooked ham

3 ounces roasted red bell peppers

Instructions

1) Preheat the Air Fryer at 360°F.

2) Roll the dough until it is around ¼-inch thick.

3) Layer in the peppers, ham, and cheese on one side of the dough and fold to seal.

4) Combine the milk and eggs to brush the dough.

5) Put the Stromboli in the basket and set the timer for 15 minutes. Check it every five minutes or so—flip the Stromboli to the other side for thorough cooking.

Yields: Four Servings

Roasted Rack of Lamb with a Macadamia Crust

Ingredients

1 clove of garlic

1 Tbsp. olive oil

Pepper and salt

1 ¾ pounds - rack of lamb

Ingredients for the Crust

3 ounces Macadamia nuts (unsalted)

1 tablespoon each

- Fresh rosemary

- Breadcrumbs

1 egg

Instructions

1) Preheat the Air Fryer to 220°F.

2) Chop the garlic clove into tiny bits. Make the garlic oil by combining the garlic and oil. Brush the lamb and flavor with salt and pepper.

3) Chop the nuts to a fine consistency in a bowl and blend in the rosemary and breadcrumbs. Beat/whip the egg in another dish.

4) Dredge the meat through the egg mixture and coat with the macadamia crust topping.

5) Place the rack of lamb in the Air Fryer basket—setting the timer for 30 minutes.

6) After the time is lapsed; raise the heat to 390°F—setting the time for an additional five minutes.

7) Take the meat from the fryer and let it rest for about ten minutes covered with some aluminum foil.

Substitutes: You can use cashews, hazelnuts, pistachios, or almonds if you would like a change of pace.

Crispy Tofu

Ingredients

2 tsp. toasted sesame oil

2 Tbsp. soy sauce

1 tsp. seasoned rice vinegar

1 block firm pressed tofu

1 tablespoon cornstarch or potato starch

Instructions

1)   Cut the tofu

   into 1-inch cubes. Preheat the Air Fryer to 370°F.

2)   In a shallow

   dish, mix the vinegar, soy sauce, oil, and tofu. Let the combination marinate

   for 15 to 30 minutes. Toss the marinated product with the cornstarch and add

   it to the AF basket.

3)   Cook for 20

   minutes, shaking the basket halfway through the cooking cycle.

Yields: Four Servings

Sides

Bread Rolls with Potato Stuffing

Ingredients

8 slices bread (white part only)

5 large potatoes

1 small bunch finely chopped coriander

2 seeded and finely chopped green chilies

½ teaspoon turmeric

2 curry leaf sprigs

½ teaspoon mustard seeds

2 finely chopped small onions

 2 tablespoons oil (frying and brushing)

Salt if desired

Instructions

1) Preheat the Air Fryer to 392°F.

2) Cut away the edges of the bread.

3) Peel the potatoes, and boil. Use one teaspoon of salt, and mash the potatoes.

4) In the meantime, on the stovetop use a skillet to combine the mustard seeds and one teaspoon of the oil. Add the onions when the seeds sputter, continue frying until they become translucent. Toss in the curry and turmeric.

5) Fry the mixture a few seconds, then add the salt, mashed potatoes; mix well, and let it cool.

6) Shape eight portions of the mixture into an oval shape. Set to the side.

7) Wet the bread with water, and press it into your palm to remove the excess water.

8) Place the oval potato into the bread and roll the bread completely around the potato mixture. Be sure they are completely sealed.

9) Brush the basket and the potato rolls with oil, and set to the side.

10) Set the Air Fryer timer for 12 to 13 minutes. Let them cook until crispy and browned.

Yields: Four Servings

Avocado Fries

Ingredients

1 large avocado

Pinch of black pepper and salt

¼ teaspoon paprika or cayenne pepper

¼ cup all-purpose flour

½ cup Panko breadcrumbs

1 beaten egg

¼ of a lemon

Instructions

1) Preheat the Air Fryer to 392°F.

2) Cut the avocado into eight slices.

3) Using three separate containers; add the salt, cayenne, pepper, and flour in one. Place the beaten egg in the second one and breadcrumbs in the third one.

4) Coat the avocado with the flour, egg, and breadcrumbs.

5) Put the avocado into the fryer basket and set the timer for six minutes.

6) They will be golden in color when ready to serve.

Enjoy with some Greek yogurt and honey or with a squeeze of fresh lemon juice.

Broccoli

Ingredients

2 Lbs. broccoli crowns

2 Tablespoons olive oil

1 teaspoon kosher salt

½ teaspoon black pepper

2 teaspoons grated lemon zest

1/3 cup Kalamata olives

¼ cup shaved Parmesan cheese

Instructions

1) Remove the stems from the broccoli and cut them into 1 to 1-1/2- inch florets. Pit and cut the olives in half.

2) Over high heat, fill a medium pan with six cups of water—bring it to boiling. Toss in the florets and cook for three to four minutes. Remove and drain. Add the pepper, salt, and oil

3) Set the AF to 400°F.

4) Place the broccoli into the basket, close the drawer, and click the timer for 15 minutes. Toss/flip at seven minutes for even browning. When done, place the broccoli in the bowl.

5) Garnish with lemon zest, olives, and cheese. Enjoy immediately.

Yields: Two to Four Servings

Fact: The Kalamata olive is a native of southern Greece which is often times preserved in olive oil or wine vinegar. It is an additional 'kick' for this treat!

Buffalo Cauliflower

Ingredients

1 cup breadcrumbs

4 cups cauliflower florets

¼cup buffalo sauce

¼ cup melted butter

For the Dip: Your favorite dressing

Instructions

1) Place the butter in a microwaveable dish; remove and whisk in the buffalo sauce.

2) Dip each of the florets in the buttery mixture; the stem does not need to have sauce. Use the stem as a handle, hold it over a cup and let the excess drip away.

3) Run the floret through the breadcrumbs to your liking. Drop them into the fryer. Cook for 14 to 17 minutes at 350°F. (The unit will not need to preheat since it is calculated in the time.)

4) You can shake the basket several times to be sure it is evenly browning. Enjoy with your favorite dip, but be sure to eat it right away because the crunchiness goes away quickly.

Note: Reheat in the oven. Don't reheat it in the microwave; it will be mushy.

Yields: Four Servings

Cheesy Potatoes

Ingredients

7 medium potatoes

½ cup grated Gruyere (semi-mature) cheese

½ cup cream

½cup milk

1 teaspoon black pepper

½ teaspoon nutmeg

Instructions

1) Peel and slice the potatoes wafer-thin. Russet potatoes work great with this recipe.

2) Preset the Air Fryer to 400°F.

3) Blend the milk and cream; add the nutmeg pepper, and salt for seasoning.

4) Generously coat the potatoes with the mixture.

5) Put the slices in an 8 x 8 dish, pouring the rest of the mixture over the potatoes.

6) Place the dish into Air Fryer and set the timer for 25 minutes.

7) Remove the dish and sprinkle the cheese over the hot potatoes.

8) Continue cooking until the cheese is melted and browned, usually an additional ten minutes.

Yields: Serves Six

French Fried Potatoes

Ingredients

6 medium peeled potatoes

2 Tbsp. olive oil

Instructions

1) Preheat the Air Fryer to 360°F.

2) Peel and cut the potatoes into 3-inch strips x ¼-inch.

3) Soak the cut potatoes for a minimum of thirty minutes in water, and drain thoroughly. Pat them dry with a towel.

4) Coat the potatoes with the oil in a large mixing container.

5) Dropthe potatoes into the cooking basket for about thirty minutes or until they are the desired doneness.

6) Shake the basket two or three times during the cooking phase.

Note: The time may vary depending on the thickness of the potatoes.

Potatoes au Gratin

Ingredients

7 Medium peeled russet potatoes

½ cup each:

- Cream

- Milk

½ teaspoon nutmeg

1 teaspoon black pepper

½ cup semi-mature (Gruyere) grated cheese

Instructions

1)   Preheat the Air Fryer to 390°F.

2)   Wash and slice the potatoes wafer-thin.

3)   Blend together the cream and milk—flavoring with some pepper, salt, and nutmeg.

4)   Use the milk mixture to coat the potatoes.

5)   Place the slices into an eight-inch baking pan/dish and pour the remainder of the milk/cream mixture on top of the potatoes.

6)   Place the heat-resistant dish onto the cooking basket—setting the timer for 25 minutes.

7)   Take the basket out and sprinkle with the cheese.

8)   Bake ten more minutes or until browned.

Note: You can use two eggs instead of milk.

Yields: Six Servings

Homemade AF Croutons

Try these with a healthy salad:

Ingredients

Stale Bread

Butter

Optional: Olive oil

Instructions

1) Preheat the Air Fryer for about two to three minutes at 248°F. (You can always adjust the time but don't hotter than 320°F.)

2) Cube some of the old bread to the sizes you want to use for your meal. Pour in the olive oil and melted butter.

3) Put the cubed bread into the basket and cook for two to three minutes.

4) Toss and cook for an additional two to three minutes.

5) Completely cool and keep in an airtight container for no more than two days.

Portobello Mushrooms

Ingredients

1.4 Oz. cubed ham (about two slices)

4 Tbsp. extra virgin olive oil

7.05 Oz. Portobello mushrooms

2 shiitake or button mushrooms

1.8 Oz. Mozzarella cheese (shredded)

1 Tbsp. chopped garlic

Optional: Ground black pepper and salt

Instructions

1) Preheat the AF cooker at 356°F.

2) Clean, cap, and remove the stalks from the mushrooms; use a couple of paper towels to pat them dry.

3) Use 1/2 of the oil to brush the Portobello mushrooms tops and place them cap side down on a baking tray lined with aluminum foil or parchment paper.

4) Divide the mushrooms and top with cheese, garlic, the other half of mushrooms—diced, and the cubed ham.

5) Flavor with the pepper and salt. Drizzle a bit of the oil over the mushrooms.

6) Cook for about 10 minutes. Garnish with some dried or fresh parsley.

The Blooming Onion

Ingredients

4 small/medium onions

4 dollops of butter

1 Tbsp. olive oil

Instructions

1) Peel the skin from the onion and cut away the top and bottom to reveal flat ends.

2) Soak the onions in salt water for four hours to take away the harshness.

3) You'll need to cut the onion as far down as you can without severing the onion. Cut four times to make eight segments.

4) Preheat the fryer to 350°F.

5) Put the onions in the fryer and drizzle with the oil—placing a dollop of butter on each one.

6) Cook in the AF until the outside is dark, usually about thirty minutes.

Note: 4 dollops is 4 heaping tablespoons

Yields: Four Servings

Onion Rings

Ingredients

For a side dish or quick snack; purchase four ounces of frozen, battered onion rings.

Instructions

1) Preheat the Air Fryer cooker to 360°F.

2) Place the frozen onion rings in the basket for ten minutes.

3) Take them from the cooker and give them a toss.

4) Reset the timer for an additional ten minutes or more if needed.

Fat-Free Fries

Ingredients

1 to 2 sweet potatoes

1 to 2 red potatoes

Sprinkle of pepper and salt

Cooking spray

Optional: Parsley

Instructions

1) Preset the Air Fryer for 356°F.

2) Peel and cut the potatoes; place in a container of water until ready for frying.

3) Use two layers of paper towels to dry the wedges and spray them with the oil.

4) Place a single layer of fries in the basket and set the timer for ten minutes.

5) After the time is up, give the fries a shake, return to the AF for an additional eight to ten minutes.

6) Take them from the fryer and season as you wish.

Garnish with a bit of parsley.

Potato Croquets

Ingredients

7 small cubed red potatoes

1 egg yolk

2 Tablespoons all-purpose flour

½ cup grated Parmesan cheese

1 Pinch Each:

- Cayenne

- Black pepper

- Salt

For the Breading:

1 cup all-purpose flour

2 Tablespoons vegetable oil

2 beaten eggs

½ cup panko

1 Pinch of nutmeg

Instructions

1) Preset the temperature on the Air Fryer to 390°F.

2) In salted water, boil the potatoes for 15 minutes, drain, and mash. Cool completely.

3) Add the flour, cheese, and egg yolk—flavoring with nutmeg, pepper, and salt,

4) Shape the filling into golf ball size.

5) Make a crumbly mixture of the breadcrumbs and oil. Put each ball into the flour mixture, the eggs, and then the panko. Roll them into cylinder shapes.

6) Put them in the cooking basket until browned—about seven to eight minutes.

Yields: It will probably take 2 batches depending on how large you made the balls.

Potato Skin Wedges

Ingredients

6 medium russet potatoes

1 ½ tsp. paprika

½ tsp. salt

2 Tbsp. canola oil

½ tsp. black pepper

Instructions

1) Thoroughly wash the potatoes under the tap. Boil the potatoes in salted water about forty minutes.

2) Cool in the refrigerator for about thirty minutes. Quarter them when cooled.

3) Combine the paprika, pepper, salt, and oil in a mixing dish. Toss the potatoes in the mixture.

4) Place in the cooking basket with the skin side down. Cook them until golden brown; about 14 to 16 minutes.

Grilled Tomatoes AF Style

Ingredients

2 tomatoes

Cooking spray

Pepper

Herbs

Instructions

1) Preheat the fryer to 320°F.

2) Wash and cut the tomatoes into halves. Spray each of them lightly with some cooking spray and place them cut side facing upwards. Sprinkle with your favorite spices—fresh or dried—including the pepper, sage, rosemary, basil, oregano, and any others of your choice.

3) Put them into the basket for 20 minutes or until they are to the doneness you want to achieve. If they are ready to enjoy—if not—cook for a few more minutes.

This would be tasty breakfast or as a side dish.

Yields: Two Servings

Chapter 5: Air Fryer Desserts

Blackberry Apricot Crumble

Ingredients

5 ½ ounces fresh blackberries

2 tablespoons lemon juice

18 ounces fresh apricots

½ cup sugar

Pinch of salt

1 cup flour

5 tablespoons cold butter

Instructions

1) Preheat the Air Fryer to 390°F.

2) Prepare an eight-inch oven dish with a small amount of cooking oil.

3) Remove the stones, cut the apricots into cubes, and place them in a container.

4) Mix the lemon juice, blackberries, and 2 tablespoons of sugar with the apricots and mix. Place the fruit in the oven dish.

5) Combine a pinch of salt, the remainder of the sugar, and the flour in a mixing container. Add 1 tablespoon cold water and the butter; using your fingertips to make a crumbly mixture.

6) Sprinkle the crumbles over the fruit and press down.

7) Place the dish into the basket and slide it into the Air Fryer for 20 minutes. It is ready when it is cooked thoroughly, and the top is browned.

Cheesecake: Lemon Ricotta

Ingredients

1 lemon

$^2/^3$ cups (150g) sugar

2 cups (500g) ricotta

2 teaspoons vanilla essence

Instructions

1) Zest and juice the lemon.

2) Preset the Air Fryer to 320°F.

3) Mix the sugar, ricotta, 1 tablespoon lemon juice as well as the zest, and the vanilla essence—stirring until fully mixed. Blend in the cornstarch and pour into the oven dish.

4) Place the dish in the Air Fryer basket and set the timer for 25 minutes.

5) The middle should be set when the cake is complexly done.

6) Leave the cheesecake on a wire rack to fully cool.

Cherry Pie

Ingredients

2 refrigerated pre-made pie crusts

1 Can cherry pie filling (21-ounces)

1 tablespoon milk

1 egg yolk

Instructions

1) Preheat the fryer to 310°F.

2) Stab holes into the crust after placing into a pie plate. Allow the excess to hang over the edges. Place in the AF for five minutes

3) Take the basket out and set the crust on the counter. Fill it with the cherries. Remove the excess crust.

4) Cut the remainder crust into ¾-inch strips placing them as a lattice across the pie.

5) Make an egg wash with the milk and egg; brush the pie.

6) Bake for fifteen minutes.

7) Serve with the ice cream of your choice.

Yields: Eight Servings

Donut Bread Pudding

Ingredients

6 glazed donuts

4 raw egg yolks

1 ½ cups whipping cream

¼ cup sugar

¾ cup frozen sweet cherries

1 teaspoon cinnamon

½ cup semi-sweet chocolate baking chips

½ cup raisins

Instructions

1) Preheat the fryer at 310°F.

2) Combine the wet ingredients in a container and combine the rest of the ingredients and mix.

3) Pour into a baking pan and cover it with foil. Place it into the basket and set the timer for 60 minutes.

4) Chill the bread pudding well before serving.

Yields: Four Servings

Fluffy Peanut Butter Marshmallow Turnovers

Ingredients

4 defrosted sheets filo pastry

4 Tbsp. chunky peanut butter

2-ounces melted butter

4 tsp. marshmallow fluff

A Pinch of sea salt

Instructions

1) Preset the temperature of the Air Fryer to 360°F.

2) Use the melted butter to brush one sheet of the filo. Put the second sheet on top and brush it also with butter.

3) Continue the process until you have completed all four sheets.

4) Cut the layers into four (4) 12-inch x 3-inch strips.

5) Place one teaspoon of the marshmallow fluff on the underside and 1 tablespoon of the peanut butter.

6) Fold the tip over the filo strip to form a triangle, making sure the filling is completely wrapped.

7) Seal the ends with a small amount of butter. Place the completed turnovers into the AF for three to five minutes.

8) When done, they will be fluffy and golden brown.

9) Add a touch of sea salt for the sweet/salty combo.

Notes: The Filo/Phyllo pastry is a little different than regular pastry. It is tissue thin and has very little fat content. It is considered okay by some bakers and is interchange the filo with regular puff pastry for turnovers.

Yields: Four Servings

Marshmallow and Yam Hand Pies

Ingredients

1 crescent dough sheet

1 (16-ounce can) candied yams

1/2 teaspoon cinnamon

1/4 teaspoon allspice

2 tablespoons marshmallow crème

1/4 teaspoon salt

1 egg, beaten

For the Maple Glaze:

1/2 cup maple syrup

½ cup confectioners' sugar

Instructions

1) Pre-set the heat on the AF to 400°F.

2) Drain the syrup from the yams. Combine the cinnamon, salt, allspice, and yams using a fork to the blend the spices and smash the yams.

3) Put the dough sheet onto a board and cut into four equal sections.

4) Spoon the filling onto the squares and add a tablespoon of the crème.

5) Use a brush to spread the egg over the edges of the dough and place the remainder of the two pieces of dough on top of the pies.

6) Use a fork to crimp the edges and cut three slits into the top for venting.

7) Place in the Air Fryer for six minutes.

8) Make the glaze from the sugar and syrup in a small dish—slowly adding the syrup—until the sugar dissolves.

9) To serve, drizzle the glaze over the warm pies and enjoy.

Yields: Four Servings.

Orange and Pineapple Fondant

Ingredients

4.2 ounces (115) g Butter

4.2 ounces (115 g) Dark chocolate

2 medium eggs

4 tablespoons castor sugar (see note below)

2 tablespoons self-rising flour

1 medium orange (rind and juice)

Instructions

1) Grease four ramekins with a small amount of oil or cooking spray.

2) Pre-set the heat in the Air Fryer to 356°F/380°C.

3) Cut and tear apart the orange and grate the orange peel.

4) Melt the butter and chocolate in a double boiler or in a glass measuring cup over a pot of hot water. Stir until it is creamy smooth.

5) Beat and whisk in the sugar and eggs—until frothy and pale. Blend in the sugar and egg mixture along with the orange bits. Add the flour and mix until well-blended.

6) Fill the ramekins about ¾ of the way full with the mixture. Cook in the Air Fryer for 12 minutes.

7) Take it from the fryer and let them rest for two minutes. (They will continue to cook.) Turn them out of the containers (upside down) into a serving platter. You can loosen the edges by tapping the ramekin gently with a butter knife.

8) The fondant will release from the center to provide you with a luscious center of pudding.

9) Garnish with some caramel sauce or vanilla ice cream.

Yields: Four Servings

How to Make Castor Sugar

Castor or caster sugar is simply granulated sugar that has been placed into a blender or food processor to make it a 'super-fine' sugar used for some recipes since it melts easier.

Instructions

1) Put the granulated sugar into the blender/food processor.

2) Pulse until it is a 'super-fine' texture—not powdery.

Pineapple Sticks with Yogurt Dip

Ingredients

¼ C. desiccated (moisture-free) coconut

1 C. vanilla yogurt

1 small sprig fresh mint

Instructions

1) Preheat the Air Fryer to 392°F.

2) Meanwhile, use similar shapes and sizes to cut the pineapple into sticks.

3) Dip the sticks into the coconut. Place the pineapple sticks in the basket and cook for ten minutes

4) *For the Dip*: Dice the mint into the yogurt.

Yields: Four Servings

Strawberry Cupcakes and Strawberry Icing

Ingredients

½ cup castor sugar

½ cup butter

2 medium eggs

½ cup self-rising flour

½ cup butter

½ teaspoon vanilla essence

½ cup icing sugar

1 tablespoon whipped cream

½ teaspoon pink food coloring

¼ cup fresh (blended) strawberries

Instructions

1) Set the Air Fryer temperature to 338°F/170°C.

2) Cream the sugar and butter in a large mixing container until it is creamy smooth.

3) Add the eggs one at a time along with the vanilla essence.

4) Blend in a small amount of flour at a time until all is completely mixed.

5) Pour them into ramekins about 80% of the way full. Place them in the Air Fryer for eight minutes.

6) *Make the Frosting:* Cream the butter and slowly mix in the icing sugar until creamy. Pour in the food coloring, (blended) strawberries, and whipped cream—mix well.

7) Take them out and use a piping bag to make the swirly frosting for a tasty 'pretty' cupcake every time.

Yields: Ten Servings

Chapter 6: Air Fryer Appetizers and Snacks

Cheesy Garlic Bread

Ingredients

5 round bread slices

5 teaspoons sun-dried tomato pesto

3 chopped garlic cloves

4 Tbsp. melted butter

1 cup grated Mozzarella cheese

Garnish Options:

- Chili flakes

- Chopped basil leaves

- oregano

Instructions

1) Preheat the Air Fryer to 356°F.

2) Cut the loaf of bread into 5 thick slices.

3) Add the butter, pesto, and cheese on the bread.

4) Put the slices in the preheated cooker for six to eight minutes.

5) Garnish with your choice of toppings.

Note: Round or Baguette bread was used for this recipe. It is recommended to add the finely chopped garlic cloves to the melted butter ahead of time for the best results.

Clams Oregano

Ingredients

2 dozen shucked clams

1 cup unseasoned breadcrumbs

4 tablespoons melted butter

3 clove minced garlic

1 teaspoon dried oregano

¼ cup chopped parsley

¼ cup grated Parmesan cheese

For the Pan:

- 1 cup sea salt

Instructions

1) Preheat the AF to 400°F.

2) Mix the oregano, parsley, parmesan cheese, breadcrumbs, and melted butter in a medium container.

3) Using a heaping tablespoon of the crumb mixture; add it to the exposed clams.

4) Fill the insert with the salt, place the clams inside and cook for three minutes.

5) Dress them up with a garnish of lemon wedges and fresh parsley.

Yields: Four Servings

Corn Tortilla Chips

Ingredients

8 corn Tortillas

1 Tbsp. olive oil

Salt if desired

Instructions

1) Preset the AF to 392°F.

2) Use a sharp knife to cut the tortillas.

3) Brush each tortilla with oil.

4) Air fry two batches for three minutes each. Sprinkle with a pinch of salt.

Crab Sticks

Ingredients

1 package 'DoDo' crab sticks

Cooking spray

Instructions

1) Take each of the sticks out of the package; find an edge, and unroll until flat.

2) Tear the sheets into 1/3 widths.

3) Place them on a plate and coat them with cooking spray.

4) Cook them in the AF for 10 minutes.

5) *Note*: If you shred the crab meat; you can cut the time in half, but they will also easily fall through the holes in the basket.

Garlic Knots

Ingredients

Marinara sauce

1 teaspoon sea salt

1 Lb. frozen pizza crust dough

1 tablespoon each:

- Garlic powder

- Grated Parmesan cheese

- Fresh chopped parsley

1) Preheat the Air Fryer to 360°F.

2) Roll out the dough until is about 1 ½ to 2-inches thick. Slice it approximately ¾-inches apart—lengthwise.

3) Roll the dough and make it into knots.

4) Add the cheese, oil, and spices in a bowl, and roll each knot in the mixture before placing it into the fry basket.

5) Set the timer for 12 minutes; flipping halfway through the cooking process (six minutes).

Serve with a dish of marinara sauce.

Yields: Four Servings

Kale Chips

Ingredients

1 Tbsp. olive oil

1 head of kale

1 tsp. Soya sauce

Instructions

1) De-stem the kale and tear it into 1 1/2 –inch pieces.

2) Rinse in cold water and thoroughly dry using some paper towels.

3) Toss the kale with the soya sauce and oil.

4) Set the Air Fryer for 200°F for two to three minutes; toss when half cooked.

Meatballs for the Party

Ingredients

2 ½ Tablespoons Worcestershire sauce

1 pound ground beef

1 Tablespoon Tabasco

¾ cup tomato ketchup

1 Tablespoon lemon juice

¼ cup vinegar

½ teaspoon dry mustard

½ cup brown sugar

3 crushed gingersnaps

Instructions

1) Combine all of the seasonings in a large mixing container—blending well.

2) Mix the beef and continue churning the ingredients.

3) Make the balls and put them in the fryer. Cook on 375°F for 15 minutes.

4) Place them on the toothpicks before serving.

Note: They are ready when the center is done, and they are crispy.

Yields: 24 Servings

Feta Triangles

Ingredients

4 ounces feta cheese

1 egg yolk

2 tablespoons finely chopped flat-leafed parsley

2 sheets frozen (defrosted) filo pastry

1 finely chopped scallion

2 tablespoons olive oil

Ground black pepper

Instructions

1) Pre-set the heat in the Air Fryer to 390°F.

2) Whisk the egg and blend in the scallion, feta, and parsley.

3) Cut the dough into three strips.

4) Place a heaping teaspoon of the feta mix underneath the pastry strip.

5) Fold the tip to form a triangle as you work your way around the strip.

6) Use a small amount of oil and brush each of the triangles before placing them in the cooker basket cooking them for three minutes.

7) Lower the heat to 360°F, and continue cooking for an additional two minutes.

Yields: Five Servings

Mozzarella Sticks

Ingredients

2 eggs

1 pound or block Mozzarella cheese

1 cup plain breadcrumbs

¼ cup white flour

3 tablespoons nonfat milk

Instructions

1) Preheat the fryer to 400°F.

2) Slice the cheese into ½-inch x 3-inch sticks.

3) Whisk the milk and egg together in one bowl, with the oil and bread crumbs in individual dishes as well.

4) Dredge the sliced cheese through the oil, egg, and breadcrumbs.

5) Place the sticks on bread tin and put them in the freezer compartment for about an hour or two.

6) Place them in small increments (don't overcrowd) into the AF basket.

7) Cook for 12 minutes.

Yields: Four Servings

Mini Quiche Wedges

Ingredients

1 (3 ½ ounces or 100 g) Frozen or ready-made pizza crust

1 egg

(1.4 ounces or 40 g) Grated cheese

½ tablespoon oil

3 tablespoons whipping cream

Fresh ground pepper

2 small pie molds

Instructions

1) Pre-set the heat on the Air Fryer to 392°F/200°C.

2) Use a bit of cooking spray to grease the molds. Line them with the dough pressing down around the edges.

3) Whisk the cheese, cream, and egg flavoring with some pepper and salt to taste. Empty the mixture into the molds.

4) Put the mold into the basket and set the timer for 12 minutes. Bake the second one the same way.

5) Take them from the molds and slice each of the quiche into six wedges.

6) You can serve at room temperature or warm.

Try these Variations:

Ingredients for Mushroom Slices

4.4 ounces or 125 g sliced mushrooms

1 teaspoon paprika

1 crushed clove of garlic

OR

Ingredients Ham and Broccoli

1.8 ounces or 50 g small broccoli florets and ham

Instructions for Ham and Broccoli

Boil the florets until tender.

Divide between each of the quiches.

Yields: Nine Servings

Spicy Pumpkin Patch Cannoli Treats for Halloween

Ingredients

4 tablespoons melted butter

8 large flour tortillas

1 cup sugar

½ cup orange sanding sugar

2 pounds whole milk ricotta

1 tablespoon ground cinnamon

2/3 cup confectioners' sugar

1 ½ cup pumpkin pie mix

½ cup mini chocolate chips

Instructions

1) Preheat the Air Fryer for three minutes at 400°F.

2) Use a pumpkin cookie cutter to make the tortillas.

3) Brush one side of the cutouts with the butter and sprinkle them with the orange sanding sugar.

4) Mix the cinnamon a regular sugar in a small dish; sprinkle over the cookies.

5) Bake the treats in batches until crispy (about three minutes).

6) Use wire racks for cooling.

7) Make the dip by using a large bowl and combining the cinnamon sugar, pumpkin pie, mix, and ricotta in a large mixing dish. Stir well.

8) Be creative and place the dip in a shallow serving platter.

9) Place the crisps into the dip to make a pumpkin patch and decorate with the chips.

Yields: Four Servings

Sweet Potato Chips

Ingredients

2 Large Sweet potatoes

1 Tbsp. olive oil

Instructions

1) Pre-set the heat in the Air Fryer to 350°F.

2) Peel and slice the potatoes into chips. It is best to slice them into the same sizes so then will cook evenly.

3) Place the potatoes into a resealable baggie and add the oil. Shake the potatoes to coat them completely.

4) Pour the sweet potatoes into the Air Fryer and cook for approximately fifteen minutes, depending on the thickness.

Index

Chapter 2: Breakfast Recipes

- Apple Dumplings

- Banana Fritters

- French Toast Sticks

- Bacon and Eggs

- Cheesy Mushroom, Ham, and Egg

- Scrambled Eggs

- Air Fryer Spinach Frittata

- Bacon Wrapped Tater Tots

- Buttermilk Biscuits

- Vegan Mini Bacon Wrapped Burritos

Chapter 3: Lunch Recipes

- Grilled Cheese Sandwich

- Cheeseburger Mini Sliders

- Pigs In A Blanket

Chicken

- AF Chicken 'Fried'

- AF Buffalo Chicken Wings

- Chinese Chicken Wings

- Country Style Chicken Tenders

- Chicken Pot Pie

- Tarragon Chicken

Beef

- Beef Roll Ups

- Air Fried Ravioli

- Roasted Veggie Pasta Salad

Chapter 4: Dinner Recipes

Chicken and Turkey Recipes

- Lemon Rosemary Chicken

- Jamaican Chicken Meatballs

- Roast Turkey Breast

- Spicy Rolled Meat

Fish and Seafood

- Salmon Patties

- Dill Salmon

- Halibut Steak With a Teriyaki Glazed Sauce

- Cajun Shrimp

- Coconut Shrimp

Beef

- Rib Steak

- Stromboli

- Roasted Rack of Lamb with a Macadamia Crust

- Crispy Tofu

Sides

- Bread Rolls with Potato Stuffing

- Avocado Fries

- Broccoli

- Buffalo Cauliflower

- Cheesy Potatoes

- French Fried Potatoes

- Potatoes au Gratin

- Homemade AF Croutons

- Portobello Mushrooms

- The Blooming Onion

- Onion Rings

- Fat-Free Fries

- Potato Croquets

- Potato Skin Wedges

- Grilled Tomatoes AF Style

Chapter 5: Air Fryer Desserts

- Blackberry Apricot Crumble

- Cheesecake: Lemon Ricotta

- Cherry Pie

- Donut Bread Pudding

- Fluffy Peanut Butter Marshmallow Turnovers

- Marshmallow and Yam Hand Pies

- Orange and Chocolate Fondant

- Pineapple Sticks with Yogurt Dip

Chapter 6: Air Fryer Appetizers and Snacks

- Cheesy Garlic Bread

- Clams Oregano

- Corn Tortilla Chips

- Crab Sticks

- Garlic Knots

- Kale Chips

- Meatballs for the Party

- Feta Triangles

- Mozzarella Sticks

- Mini Quiche Wedges

- Spicy Pumpkin Patch Cannoli Treats for Halloween

- Sweet Potato Chips

PART IV

Chapter 1: Keto Basics

Benefits of Increased Metabolism

One of the best ways to learn the meaning of a scientific term is to break it down to its roots. When we break down ketogenic, we see it is comprised of two words: keto and genic. Ketones are fat-based molecules that the body breaks down when it is using fat as its energy source. When used as a suffix, "genic" means "causing, forming, or producing." So, we put these terms together, and we have "ketogenic," or simply put, "causing fat burn." Ergo, the theory behind ketogenic dieting is: when a person reduces the amount of sugar and carbohydrates they consume, the body will begin to breakdown fat it already has in stores all over the body. When your body is cashing in on these stores, it is in a ketogenic state, or "ketosis." When your body consumes food, it naturally seeks carbohydrates for the purpose of breaking them down and using them as fuel. Adversely, a ketogenic cleanse trains your body to use fats for energy instead. This is achieved by lowering the amount of ingested carbohydrates and increasing the amount of ingested fats, which in turn boosts your metabolism.

 Only recently has a low carb- high-fat diet plan emerged into the public eye. It is a sharp contrast to the traditional dieting style that emphasizes calorie counting. For many years it was overlooked that crash diets neglect the most important aspect of dieting: food is fuel. A diet is not meant to be treated as a once a year go to method in order to shed holiday weight in January. Rather, a diet is a lifestyle; it is a consistent pattern of how individual fuels their body. A ten day ketogenic cleanse is the perfect way to begin forming healthy eating habits that over time become second nature. If you are tired of losing weight just to gain it all back, never fear. We firmly believe that you can accomplish anything you put your mind to, including living a healthy life! You, like hundreds of others, can successfully accomplish a ketogenic cleanse and change the way you see health, fitness, and life along the way. So let's hit the books and get that metabolism working!

Benefits of Cleansing

In addition to increased metabolism and fat loss, ketogenic cleansing allows your body naturally rid itself of harmful toxins and wasteful substances. In today's modern world, food is overrun and polluted by genetically modified hormones, artificial flavors and coloring, and copious amounts of unnecessary sugars. Ketogenic cleansing eliminates bread, grains, and many other foods that are most affected by today's modern industrialization. Due to the high amount of naturally occurring foods used in a ketogenic cleanse, the body is able to obtain many vitamins and minerals that are not prevalent in a high carb diet. When the body is consuming sufficient amounts of necessary vitamins and minerals, it is able to heal itself and maintain a healthy immune system. Cleansing your body is one of the best ways to achieve, and maintain pristine health.

Chapter 2: Meal Plan Madness

One of the best ways to stay motivated, when dieting, is to find a meal plan that is easy to follow and easy on the budget. Ketogenic meals are designed to be filling while keeping within the perimeters of low-carb, high-fat guidelines. Ideally, you want to aim for 70% fats, 25% protein, and 5% carbohydrates in your diet. As long as the materials you use to build your meals are low in carbs and high in fats, feel free to experiment and find what is right for you. Each and every one of us is different, and that's okay. After all, this meal plan is for YOU!

Below is a ten-day meal plan, designed with a busy schedule in mind, which will not break the bank! All of these meals can be prepared in 30 minutes or less, and many of them are much quicker than that! There is also a list of ingredients for each meal located in the recipe chapter so you can go to the grocery store knowing exactly what you need!

	Breakfast	**Lunch**	**Dinner**
Day 1	**California Chicken Omelet** • Fat: 32 grams • 10 minutes to prepare • Protein: 25 grams • 10 minutes of cooking • Net carbs: 4 grams	**Cobb Salad** • Fat: 48 grams • 10 minutes to prepare • Protein: 43 grams • 0 minutes of cooking • Net carbs: 3 grams	**Chicken Peanut Pad Thai** • Fat: 12 grams • 15 minutes to prepare • Protein: 30 grams • 15 minutes of cooking • Net carbs: 2 g
Day 2	**Easy Blender Pancakes** • Fat: 29 grams • 5 minutes to prepare • Protein: 41 grams • 10 minutes of cooking • Net carbs: 4 grams	**Sardine Stuffed Avocados** • Fat: 29 grams • 10 minutes to prepare • Protein: 27 grams • 0 minutes of cooking • Net Carbs: 5 grams	**Chipotle Fish Tacos** • Fat: 20 grams • 5 minutes to prepare • Protein: 24 grams • 15 minutes of cooking • Net carbs: 5 grams

Day 3	**Steak and Eggs** • Fat: 36 grams • 10 minutes to prepare • Protein: 47 grams • 5 minutes of cooking • Net carbs: 3 grams	**Low-Carb Smoothie Bowl** • Fat 35 grams • 5 minutes to prepare • Protein: 20 grams • 0 minutes of cooking • Net carbs: 5 grams	**Avocado Lime Salmon** • Fat: 27 grams • 20 minutes to prepare • Protein: 37 grams • 10 minutes of cooking • Net carbs: 5 grams
KEEP IT UP!!!	During the course of your plan, especially around days 3 and 4, you may begin to feel like you don't have it in you. You may have thoughts telling you that you cannot last for ten days on this type pf cleanse. Do not allow feelings of discouragement bother you because, guess what? We all feel that way sometimes! A ketogenic diet causes your body to process energy like it never has before. Keep pressing on! Your body will thank you and so will you!		
Day 4	**Low-Carb Smoothie Bowl** • Fat: 35 grams • 5 minutes to prepare • Protein: 35 grams • 0 minutes of cooking • Net carbs: 4 grams	**Pesto Chicken Salad** • Fat: 27 grams • 5 minutes to prepare • Protein: 27 grams • 10 minutes of cooking • Net carbs: 3 g	**Siracha Lime Flank Steak** • Fat: 32 grams • 5 minutes to prepare • Protein: 48 grams • 10 minutes of cooking • Net Carbs: 5 g
Day 5	**Feta and Pesto Omelet** • Fat: 46 grams • 5 minutes of preparation • Protein: 30 grams • 5 minutes of cooking • Net carbs: 2.5 grams	**Roasted Brussel Sprouts** • Fat: 21 grams • 5 minutes to prepare • Protein: 21 grams • 30 minutes of cooking • Net carbs: 4 grams	**Low carb Sesame Chicken** • Fat: 36 grams • 15 minutes to prepare • Protein: 41 grams • 15 minutes of cooking • Net carbs: 4 grams
Day 6	**Raspberry Cream Crepes** • Fat: 40 grams	**Shakshuka** • Fat: 34 grams • Protein 35	**Sausage in a Pan** • Fat: 38 grams • 10 minutes of

	• 5 minutes of preparation • Net carbs: 8 grams • 15 minutes of cooking • Protein 15 grams	grams • Net carbs: 4 grams • 10 minutes of preparation • 10 minutes of cooking	preparation • Protein: 30 grams • 25 minutes of cooking • Net Carbs: 4 grams
Day 7	**Green Monster Smoothie** • Fat: 25 grams • 5 minutes of preparation • Protein: 30 grams • 0 minutes of cooking • Net Carbs: 3 grams	**Tuna Tartare** • Fat: 24 grams • 15 minutes of preparation • Protein: 56 grams • 0 minutes of cooking • Net Carbs: 4 grams	**Pesto Chicken Salad** • Fat: 27 grams • 5 minutes of preparation • Protein: 27 grams • 10 minutes of cooking • Net carbs: 3 grams
ALMOST THERE!!	By now, you can be certain you are seeing physical results such as reduced body fat and more energy! You are doing a fantastic job and you only have three days left! Keep up the good work, you owe it to yourself.		
Day 8	**Shakshuka** • Fat: 34 grams • 10 minutes of preparation • Protein 35 grams • 10 minutes of cooking • Net carbs: 4 grams	**Grilled Halloumi Salad** • Fat: 47 grams • 15 minutes of preparation • Protein: 21 grams • 0 minutes of cooking • Net carbs: 2 grams	**Keto Quarter Pounder** • Fat: 34 grams • 10 minutes of preparation • Protein: 25 grams • 8 minutes of cooking • Net carbs: 4 grams
Day 9	**Easy Blender Pancakes** • Fat: 29 grams • 5 minutes of preparation • Protein: 41 grams	**Broccoli Bacon Salad** • Fat: 31 grams • 15 minutes of preparation • Protein: 10	**Sardine Stuffed Avocados** • Fat: 29 grams • 10 minutes to prepare • Protein: 27

	• 10 minutes of cooking • Net carbs: 4 grams	grams • 6 minutes of cooking • Net carbs: 5 grams	grams • 0 minutes to cook • Net Carbs: 5 grams
Day 10	**California Chicken Omelet** • Fat 32 grams • 10 minutes to prepare • Protein 25 grams • 10 minutes of cooking • Net carb: 3 grams	**Shrimp Scampi** • Fat: 21 grams • 5 minutes to prepare • Protein: 21 grams • 30 minutes of cooking • Net carbs: 4 grams	**Tuna Tartare** • Fat: 36 grams • 15 minutes to prepare • Protein: 41 grams • 15 minutes of cooking • Net carbs: 4 grams
YOU DID IT!!	Congratulations! You have successfully completed a 10 day ketogenic cleanse. By now your body has adjusted to its new source of energy, expelled dozens of harmful toxins, and replenished itself with many vitamins and minerals it may have been lacking. Way to go on a job well done!		

Chapter 3: Breakfast Is For Champions

Breakfast is by far the most important meal of the day for one reason: it set the tone for the rest of your day. In order to hit the ground running, it is vital that one starts each day with foods that fuel an energetic and productive day. This chapter contains ten ketogenic breakfast ides that will have you burning fat and conquering your day like you never imagined.

1. California Chicken Omelet

- This recipe requires 10 minutes of preparation, 10 minutes of cooking time and serves 1
- Net carbs: 4 grams
- Protein: 25 grams
- Fat : 32 grams

What you will need:

- Mayo (1 tablespoon)
- Mustard (1 teaspoon)
- Campari tomato
- Eggs (2 large beaten)
- Avocado (one fourth, sliced)
- Bacon (2 slices cooked and chopped)
- Deli chicken (1 ounce)

What to do:

1. Place a skillet on the stove over a burner set to a medium heat and let it warm before adding in the eggs and seasoning as needed.
2. Once eggs are cooked about halfway through, add bacon, chicken, avocado, tomato, mayo, and mustard on one side of the eggs.
3. Fold the omelet onto its self, cover and cook for 5 additional minutes.
4. Once eggs are fully cooked and all ingredients are warm, through the center, your omelet is ready.
5. Bon apatite!

2. Steak and Eggs with Avocado

- This recipe requires 10 minutes of preparation, 5 minutes of cooking time and serves 1
- Net Carbs: 3 grams
- Protein: 44 grams
- Fat: 36 grams

What you will need:

- Salt and pepper
- Avocado (one fourth, sliced)
- Sirloin steak (4 ounce)
- Eggs (3 large)
- Butter (1 tablespoon)

What to do:

1. Melt the tablespoon of butter in a pan and fry all 3 eggs to desired doneness. Season the eggs with salt and pepper.
2. In a different pan, cook the sirloin steak to your preferred taste and slice it into thin strips. Season the steak with salt and pepper.
3. Sever your prepared steak and eggs with slices of avocado.
4. Enjoy!

3. Pancakes an a Blender

- This recipe requires 5 minutes of preparation, 10 minutes of cooking time and serves 1
- Net Carbs: 4 grams
- Protein: 41 grams
- Fat: 29 grams

What you will need:

- Whey protein powder (1 scoop)
- Eggs (2 large)
- Cream cheese (2 ounces)
- Just a pinch of cinnamon and a pinch of salt

What to do:

1. Combine cream cheese, eggs, protein powder, cinnamon, and salt into a blender. Blend for 10 seconds and let stand.
2. While letting batter stand, warm a skillet over medium heat.
3. Pour about ¼ of the batter onto warmed skillet and let cook. When bubbles begin to emerge on the surface, flip the pancake.
4. Once flipped, cook for 15 seconds. Repeat until remainder of the batter is used up.
5. Top with butter and/ or sugar- free maple syrup and you are all set!
6. Chow time!

4. Low Carb Smoothe Bowl

- Net Carbs: 4 grams
- Protein: 35 grams
- Fat: 35 grams
- Takes 5 minutes to prepare and serves 1.

What you will need:

- Spinach (1 cup)
- Almond milk (half a cup)
- Coconut oil (1 tablespoon)
- Low carb protein powder (1 scoop)
- Ice cubes (2 cubes)
- Whipping cream (2 T)
- Optional toppings can include: raspberries, walnuts, shredded coconut, or chia seeds

What to do:

1. Place spinach in blender. Add almond milk, cream, coconut oil, and ice. Blend until thoroughly and evenly combined.
2. Pour into bowl.
3. Top with toppings or stir lightly into smoothie.
4. Treat yourself!

5. Feta and Pesto Omelet

- This recipe requires 5 minutes of preparation, 5 minutes of cooking time and serves 1
- Net Carbs: 2.5 grams
- Protein: 30 grams
- Fat: 46 grams

What you will need:

- Butter (1 tablespoon)
- Eggs (3 large)
- Heavy cream (1 tablespoon)
- Feta cheese (1 ounce)
- Basil pesto (1 teaspoon)
- Tomatoes (optional)

What to do:

1. Heat pan and melt butter.
2. Beat eggs together with heavy whipping cream (will give eggs a fluffy consistency once cooked).
3. Pour eggs in pan and cook until almost done, add feta and pesto to on half of eggs.
4. Fold omelet and cook for an additional 4-5 minutes.
5. Top with feta and tomatoes, and eat up!

6. Crepes with Cream and Raspberries

- This recipe requires 5 minutes of preparation, 15 minutes of cooking time and serves 2
- Net Carbs: 8 grams
- Protein: 15 grams
- Fat: 40 grams

What you will need:

- Raspberries (3 ounces, fresh or frozen)
- Whole Milk Ricotta (half a cup and 2 tablespoons)
- Erythritol (2 tablespoons)
- Eggs (2 large)
- Cream Cheese (2 ounces)
- Pinch of salt
- Dash of Cinnamon
- Whipped cream and sugar- free maple syrup to go on top

What to do:

1. In a blender, blend cream cheese, eggs, erythritol, salt, and cinnamon for about 20 seconds, or until there are no lumps of cream cheese.
2. Place a pan on a burner turned to a medium heat before coating in cooking spray. Add 20 percent of your batter to the pan in a thin layer. Cook crepe until the underside becomes slightly darkened. Carefully flip the crepe and let the reverse side cook for about 15 seconds.
3. Repeat step 3 until all batter is used.
4. Without stacking the crepes, allow them to cool for a few minutes.
5. After the crepes have cool, place about 2 tablespoons of ricotta cheese in the center of each crepe.
6. Throw in a couple of raspberries and fold the side to the middle.
7. Top those off with some whipped cream and sugar- free maple syrup and…

8. Viola! You're a true chef! Indulge in your creation!

7. Green Monster Smoothie

- This recipe requires 10 minutes of preparation, 0 minutes of cooking time and serves 1
- Net Carbs: 4 grams
- Protein: 30 grams
- Fat: 25 grams

What you will need:

- Almond milk (one and a half cups)
- Spinach (one eighth of a cup)
- Cucumber (fourth of a cup)
- Celery (fourth of a cup)
- Avocado (fourth of a cup)
- Coconut oil (1 tablespoon)
- Stevia (liquid, 10 drops)
- Whey Protein Powder (1 scoop)

What to do:

1. In a blender, blend almond milk and spinach for a few pulses.
2. Add remaining ingredients and blend until thoroughly combined.
- Add optional matcha powder, if desired, and enjoy!

Chapter 4: Lunch Crunch

Eating a healthy lunch when you are limited on time due to, work, school, or taking care of your kids can be a tumultuous task. Thankfully, we have compiled a list of eight quick and easy recipes to accompany the ten day meal plan laid out in chapter 2! Many find it advantageous, especially if you work throughout the week, to prepare you meals ahead of time. Thankfully, these lunch recipes are also easy to pack and take on the go!

1. Off The Cobb Salad

- Net carbs: 3 grams
- Protein: 43 grams
- Fat: 48 grams
- Takes 10 minutes to prepare and serves 1.

What you will need:
- Spinach (1 cup)
- Egg (1, hard-boiled)
- Bacon (2 strips)
- Chicken breast (2 ounces)
- Campari tomato (one half of tomato)
- Avocado (one fourth, sliced)
- White vinegar (half of a teaspoon)
- Olive oil (1 tablespoon)

What to do:
1. Cook chicken and bacon completely and cut or slice into small pieces.
2. Chop remaining ingredients into bite size pieces.
3. Place all ingredients, including chicken and bacon, in a bowl, toss ingredients in oil and vinegar.
4. Enjoy!

2. Avocado and Sardines

- Net Carbs: 5 grams
- Protein: 27 grams
- Fat: 52 grams
- Takes 10 minutes to prepare and serves 1.

What you will need:

- Fresh lemon juice (1 tablespoon)
- Spring onion or chives (1 or small bunch)
- Mayonnaise (1 tablespoon)
- Sardines (1 tin, drained)
- Avocado (1 whole, seed removed)
- Turmeric powder (fourth of a teaspoon) or freshly ground turmeric root (1 teaspoon)
- Salt (fourth of a teaspoon)

What to do:

1. Begin by cutting the avocado in half and removing its seed.
2. Scoop out about half the avocado and set aside (shown below).
3. In small bowl, mash drained sardines with fork.
4. Add onion (or chives), turmeric powder, and mayonnaise. Mix well.
5. Add removed avocado to sardine mixture.
6. Add lemon juice and salt.
7. Scoop the mixture into avocado halves.
8. Dig   in!

3. Chicken Salad A La Pesto

- This recipe requires 5minutes of preparation, 10 minutes of cooking time and serves 4

- Net Carbs: 3 grams

- Protein: 27 grams

- Fat: 27 grams

What you will need:

- Garlic pesto (2 tablespoons)
- Mayonnaise (fourth of a cup)
- Grape tomatoes (10, halved)
- Avocado (1, cubed)
- Bacon (6 slices, cooked crisp and crumbled)
- Chicken (1 pound, cooked and cubed)
- Romaine lettuce (optional)

What to do:

1. Combine all ingredients in a large mixing bowl.
2. Toss gently to spread mayonnaise and pesto evenly throughout.
3. If desired, wrap in romaine lettuce for a low-carb BLT chicken wrap.
4. Bon apatite!

4. Bacon and Roasted Brussel Sprouts

- This recipe requires 5 minutes of preparation, 30 minutes of cooking time and serves 4
- Net Carbs: 4 grams
- Protein: 15 grams
- Fat: 21 grams

What you will need:

- Bacon (8 strips)
- Olive oil (2 tablespoons)
- Brussel sprouts (1 pound, halved)
- Salt and pepper

What to do:

1. Preheat oven to 375 degrees Fahrenheit.
2. Gently mix Brussel sprouts with olive oil, salt, and pepper.
3. Spread Brussel sprouts evenly onto a greased baking sheet.
4. Bake in oven for 30 minutes. Shake the pan about halfway through to mix the Brussel sprout halves up a bit.
5. While Brussel sprouts are in the oven, fry bacon slices on stovetop.
6. When bacon is fully cooked, let cool and chop it into bite size pieces.
7. Combine bacon and Brussel sprouts in a bowl and you're finished!
8. Feast!!

5. Grilled Halloumi Salad

- Net Carbs: 7 grams
- Protein: 21 grams
- Fat: 47 grams
- Takes 15 minutes to prepare and serves 1.

What you will need:

- Chopped walnuts (half of an ounce)
- Baby arugula (1 handful)
- Grape tomatoes (5)
- Cucumber (1)
- Halloumi cheese (3 ounces)
- Olive oil (1 teaspoon)
- Balsamic vinegar (half of a teaspoon)
- A pinch of salt

What to do:

1. Slice halloumi cheese into slices 1/3 of an in thick.
2. Grill cheese for 3 to 5 minutes, until you see grill lines, on each side.
3. Wash and cut veggies into bite size pieces, place in salad bowl.
4. Add rinsed baby arugula and walnuts to veggies.
5. Toss in olive oil, balsamic vinegar, and salt.
6. Place grilled halloumi on top of veggies and your lunch is ready!
7. Eat those greens and get back to work!

6. Bacon Broccoli Salad

- This recipe requires 15 minutes of preparation, 6 minutes of cooking time and serves 5.
- Net Carbs: 5 grams
- Protein: 10 grams
- Fat: 31 grams

What you will need:

- Sesame oil (half of a teaspoon)
- Erythritol (1 and a half tablespoons) or stevia to taste
- White vinegar (1 tablespoon)
- Mayonnaise (half of a cup)
- Green onion (three fourths of an ounce)
- Bacon (fourth of a pound)
- Broccoli (1 pound, heads and stalks cut and trimmed)

What to do:

1. Cook bacon and crumble into bits.
2. Cut broccoli into bite sized pieces.
3. Slice scallions.
4. Mix mayonnaise, vinegar, erythritol (or stevia), and sesame oil, to make the dressing.
5. Place broccoli and bacon bits in a bowl and toss with dressing.
6. Viola!

7. Tuna Avocado Tartare

- Net Carbs: 4 grams
- Protein: 56 grams
- Fat: 24 grams
- Takes 15 minutes to prepare and serves 2.

What you will need:

- Sesame seed oil (2 tablespoons)
- Sesame seeds (1 teaspoon)
- Cucumbers (2)
- Lime (half of a whole lime)
- Mayonnaise (1 tablespoon)
- Sriracha (1 tablespoon)
- Olive oil (2 tablespoons)
- Jalapeno (one half of whole jalapeno)
- Scallion (3 stalks)
- Avocado (1)
- Tuna steak (1 pound)
- Soy sauce (1 tablespoon)

What to do:

1. Dice tuna and avocado into ¼ inch cubes, place in bowl.

2. Finely chop scallion and jalapeno, add to bowl.

3. Pour olive oil, sesame oil, siracha, soy sauce, mayonnaise, and lime into bowl.

4. Using hands, toss all ingredients to combine evenly. Using a utensil may breakdown avocado, which you want to remain chunky, so it is best to use your hands.

5. Top with sesame seeds and serve with a side of sliced cucumber.

6. There's certainly something fishy about this recipe, but it tastes great! Enjoy!

8. Warm Spinach and Shrimp

- This recipe requires 15 minutes of preparation, 6 minutes of cooking time and serves 5.

- Fat: 24 grams

- Protein: 36 grams

- Net Carbs: 3 grams

- Takes10 minutes to prepare, 5 minutes to cook, and serves 2.

What you will need:

- Spinach (2 handfuls)

- Parmesan (half a tablespoon)

- Heavy cream (1 tablespoon)

- Olive oil (1 tablespoon)

- Butter (2 tablespoons)

- Garlic (3 cloves)

- Onion (one fourth of whole onion)

- Large raw shrimp (about 20)

- Lemon (optional)

What to do:

1. Place peeled shrimp in cold water.

2. Chop onions and garlic into fine pieces.

3. Heat oil, in pan, over medium heat. Cook shrimp in oil until lightly pink (we do not want them fully cooked here). Remove shrimp from oil and set aside.

4. Place chopped onions and garlic into pan, cook until onions are translucent. Add a dash of salt.

5. Add butter, cream, and parmesan cheese. Stir until you have a smooth sauce.

6. Let sauce cook for about 2 minutes so it will thicken slightly.

7. Place shrimp back into pan and cook until done. This should take no longer than 2 or 3 minutes. Be careful not to overcook the shrimp, it will become dry and tough!

8. Remove shrimp and sauce from pan and replace with spinach. Cook spinach VERY briefly

9. Place warmed spinach onto a plate.

10. Pour shrimp and sauce over bed of spinach, squeeze some lemon on top, if you like, and you're ready to chow down!

Chapter 5: Thinner by Dinner

It's the end of the day and you are winding down from a hard day's work. Your body does not require a lot of energy while you sleep; therefore, dinner will typically consist of less fat and more protein.

1. Chicken Pad Thai

- Net Carbs: 7 grams
- Protein: 30 grams
- Fat: 12 grams
- Takes 15 minutes to prepare, 15 minutes to cook, and serves 4.

What you will need:

- Peanuts (1 ounce)
- Lime (1 whole)
- Soy sauce (2 tablespoons)
- Egg (1 large)
- Zucchini (2 large)
- Chicken thighs (16 ounces, boneless and skinless)
- Garlic (2 cloves, minced)
- White onion (1,chopped)
- Olive oil (1 tablespoon)
- Chili flakes (optional)

What to do:

1. Over medium heat, cook olive oil and onion until translucent. Add the garlic and cook about three minutes (until fragrant).
2. Cook chicken in pan for 5 to 7 minutes on each side (until fully cooked). Remove chicken from heat and shred it using a couple of forks.
3. Cut ends off zucchini and cut into thin noodles. Set zucchini noodles aside.
4. Next, scramble the egg in the pan.
5. Once the egg is fully cooked, and the zucchini noodles and cook for about 2 minutes.

6. Add the previously shredded chicken to the pan.

7. Give it some zing with soy sauce, lime juice, peanuts, and chili flakes.

8. Time to eat!

2. Chipotle Style Fish Tacos

- Fat: 20 grams
- Protein: 24 grams
- Net Carbs: 7 grams
- Takes 5 minutes to prepare, 15 minutes to cook, and serves 4.

What you will need:

- Low carb tortillas (4)
- Haddock fillets (1 pound)
- Mayonnaise (2 tablespoons)
- Butter (2 tablespoons)
- Chipotle peppers in adobo sauce (4 ounces)
- Garlic (2 cloves, pressed)
- Jalapeño (1 fresh, chopped)
- Olive oil (2 tablespoons)
- Yellow onion (half of an onion, diced)

What to do:

1. Fry diced onion (until translucent) in olive oil in a high sided pan, over medium- high heat.
2. Reduce heat to medium, add jalapeno and garlic. Cook while stir for another two minutes.
3. Chop the chipotle peppers and add them, along with the adobo sauce, to the pan.
4. Add the butter, mayo, and fish fillets to the pan.
5. Cook the fish fully while breaking up the fillets and stirring the fish into other ingredients.
6. Warm tortillas for 2 minutes on each side.
7. Fill tortillas with fishy goodness and eat up!

3. Salmon with Avocado Lime Sauce

- Net Carbs: 5 grams

- Protein: 37 grams

- Fat: 27 grams

- Takes 20 minutes to prepare, 10 minutes to cook, and serves 2.

What you will need:

- Salmon (two 6 ounce fillets)
- Avocado (1 large)
- Lime (one half of a whole lime)
- Red onion (2 tablespoons, diced)
- Cauliflower (100 grams)

What to do:

1. Chop cauliflower in a blender or food processor then cook it in a lightly oiled pan, while covered, for 8 minutes. This will make the cauliflower rice-like.

2. Next, blend the avocado with squeezed lime juice in the blender or processor until smooth and creamy.

3. Heat some oil in a skillet and cook salmon (skin side down first) for 4 to 5 minute. Flip the fillets and cook for an additional 4 to 5 minutes.

4. Place salmon fillet on a bed of your cauliflower rice and top with some diced red onion.

4. Siracha Lime Steak

- Net Carbs: 5 grams
- Protein: 48 grams
- Fat: 32 grams
- Takes 5 minutes to prepare, 10 minutes to cook, and serves 2.

What you will need:

- Vinegar (1 teaspoon)
- Olive oil (2 tablespoons)
- Lime (1 whole)
- Sriracha (2 tablespoons)
- Flank steak (16 ounce)
- Salt and pepper

What to do:

1. Season steak, liberally, with salt and pepper. Place on baking sheet, lined with foil, and broil in oven for 5 minutes on each side (add another minute or two for a well done steak). Remove from oven, cover, and set aside.

2. Place sriracha in small bowl and squeeze lime into it. Whisk in salt, pepper, and vinegar.

3. Slowly pour in olive oil.

4. Slice steak into thin slices, lather on your sauce, and enjoy!

5. Feel free to pair this recipe with a side of greens such as asparagus or broccoli.

5. Low Carb Sesame Chicken

- Net Carbs: 4 grams

- Protein: 45 grams

- Fat: 36 grams

- Takes 15minutes to prepare, 15 minutes to cook, and serves 2.

What you will need:

- Broccoli (three fourths of a cup, cut bite size)

- Xanthan gum (fourth of a teaspoon)

- Sesame seeds (2 tablespoons)

- Garlic (1 clove)

- Ginger (1 cm cube)

- Vinegar (1 tablespoon)

- Brown sugar alternative (Sukrin Gold is a good one) (2 tablespoons)

- Soy sauce (2 tablespoons)

- Toasted sesame seed oil (2 tablespoons)

- Arrowroot powder or corn starch (1 tablespoon)

- Chicken thighs (1poundcut into bite sized pieces)

- Egg (1 large)

- Salt and pepper

- Chives (optional)

What to do:

1. First we will make the batter by combining the egg with a tablespoon of arrowroot powder (or cornstarch). Whisk well.

2. Place chicken pieces in batter. Be sure to coat all sides of chicken pieces with the batter.

3. Heat one tablespoon of sesame oil, in a large pan. Add chicken pieces to hot oil and fry. Be gentle when flipping the chicken, you want to keep the batter from falling off. It should take about 10 minutes for them to cook fully.

4. Next, make the sesame sauce. In a small bowl, combine soy sauce, brown sugar alternative, vinegar, ginger, garlic, sesame seeds, and the remaining tablespoon of toasted sesame seed oil. Whisk very well.

5. Once the chicken is fully cooked, add broccoli and the sesame sauce to pan and cook for an additional 5 minutes.

6. Spoon desired amount into a bowl, top it off with some chopped chives, and relish in some fine dining at home!

6. Pan 'O Sausage

- Net Carbs: 4 grams

- Protein: 30 grams

- Fat: 38 grams

- Takes 10 minutes to prepare, 25 minutes to cook, and serves 2.

What you will need:

- Basil (half a teaspoon)

- Oregano (half a teaspoon)

- White onion (1 tablespoon)

- Shredded mozzarella (fourth of a cup)

- Parmesan cheese (fourth of a cup)

- Vodka sauce (half a cup)

- Mushrooms (4 ounces)

- Sausage (3 links)

- Salt (fourth of a teaspoon)

- Red pepper (fourth of a teaspoon, ground)

What to do:

1. Preheat oven to 350 degrees Fahrenheit.

2. Heat an iron skillet over medium flame. When skillet is hot, cook sausage links until almost thoroughly cooked.

3. While sausage is cooking, slice mushrooms and onion.

4. When sausage is almost fully cooked, remove links from heat and place mushrooms and onions in skillet to brown.

5. Cut sausage into pieces about ½ inch thick and place pieces in pan.

6. Season skillet contents with oregano, basil, salt, and red pepper.

7. Add vodka sauce and parmesan cheese. Stir everything together.

8. Place skillet in oven for 15 minutes. Sprinkle mozzarella on top a couple minutes before removing dish from oven.

9. Once 15 minutes is up, remove skillet from the oven and let cool for a few minutes.

10. Dinner   time!

7. Quarter Pounder Keto Burger

- Net Carbs: 4 grams
- Protein: 25 grams
- Fat: 34 grams
- Takes 10 minutes to prepare, 8 minutes to cook, and serves 2.

What you will need:

- Basil (half a teaspoon)
- Cayenne (fourth a teaspoon)
- Crushed red pepper (half a teaspoon)
- Salt (half a teaspoon)
- Lettuce (2 large leaves)
- Butter (2 tablespoons)
- Egg (1 large)
- Sriracha (1 tablespoon)
- Onion (fourth of whole onion)
- Plum tomato (half of whole tomato)
- Mayo (1 tablespoon)
- Pickled jalapenos (1 tablespoon, sliced)
- Bacon (1 strip)
- Ground beef (half a pound)
- Bacon (1 strip)

What to do:

1. Knead mean for about three minute.
2. Chop bacon, jalapeno, tomato, and onion into fine pieces. (shown below)
3. Knead in mayo, sriracha, egg, and chopped ingredients, and spices into meat.
4. Separate meat into four even pieces and flatten them (not thinly, just press on the tops to create a flat surface). Place a tablespoon of butter on top of two of the meat pieces. Take the pieces that do not have butter of them and set them on top of the buttered ones (basically creating a butter and meat sandwich). Seal the sides together, concealing the butter within.

5. Throw the patties on the grill (or in a pan) for about 5 minutes on each side. Caramelize some onions if you want too!

6. Prepare large leaves of lettuce by spreading some mayo onto them. Once patties are finished, place them on one half of the lettuce, add your desired burger toppings, and fold the other half over of the lettuce leaf over the patty.

Burger time!

BREAKFAST

Breakfast Recipes To Start Your Day Strong

Sconey Sconey Sunday – 6 SmartPoints Per Serving

This breakfast dish is best made on the weekend and enjoyed all week long. This breakfast should be filling in the moment due to the fluffiness of the scone and should keep you satisfied all morning because of the liberal use of peaches. If you are new to baking, or just a little bit afraid of your own oven, this is a great recipe to start with. There is no need to wait for any ingredients to rise and it builds the foundation for many other scone recipes. You can replace the peach with blueberries, banana, apple, etc. Try and experiment to find what you like most.

Ready in 25 Minutes

10 minutes to prep and 15 minutes to cook

Ingredients (serves 4):

2/3 cups of all purpose flour

½ teaspoon of baking powder

½ teaspoon of baking soda

1 teaspoon of powdered sugar

2 tablespoons of sugar

½ teaspoon of half and half

1 teaspoon of margarine

1/3 cup of vanilla yogurt (I highly recommend Stoneyfield for the best results)

1 teaspoon of salt

3 tablespoons of chopped peaches (if you are using canned peaches, make sure you drain the peaches and give the peaches some time to dry. I recommend not using canned as they tend to contain additional sugars that add unnecessary calories and distort the flavor of the peaches)

Non-stick cooking spray

Step 1:

Preheat the oven to 400 degrees F or 205 degrees C

Step 2:

Take a medium size mixing bowl and add the flour, sugar (not powdered), baking powder, baking soda, and salt. Mix the ingredients and add in the margarine while doing so. The margarine can be difficult to work with so you may want to heat it up in a microwave for 15 seconds, or alternatively cut the margarine into small pieces. Only move onto step 4 when you have a consistent base in the bowl – the margarine should be fully mixed in.

Step 3:

Add the yogurt and the peaches, mixing while you do so.

Step 4:

Take a large piece of wax paper and empty the contents of the bowl onto the paper. Knead the dough for 3-4 minutes. Many are unsure of how to knead the dough, so think about it as folding the dough over itself over and over.

Step 5:

Coat a large baking tray with non-stick spray and form the scones on the tray. The scones look best when shaped like triangles. The exact size of the scones is not as important as making sure the scones are of equal size. This recipe usually yields between 4 and 6 scones. Make sure the dough is firmly pressed against the baking tray. Bake for 12-15 minutes on the center oven rack.

Step 6:

Remove the scones from the oven and while still hot, paint the scones with milk. This should look like they are slightly moist from the milk. Use this moisture to spread the powdered sugar over the scones. You can serve these right away and they will last about one week at room temperature.

10 Minute Fried Toast – 3 SmartPoints Per Serving

Yes this recipe is truly just a variation of French Toast but I want to stress the importance of a hot breakfast and that it doesn't take too much time to prepare one. This dish can be enjoyed even on a weekday before work and with a little practice you can cut down on the prep time dramatically. This is a dish I commonly make for my daughter before school and it can be made almost as fast as some simple scrambled eggs.

Ready in 10 Minutes

5 minutes to prep and 5 minutes to cook

Ingredients (serves 2):

4 egg whites

6 slices of wheat bread (you'll have lots of options of bread but I suggest looking at the low calorie version. I have switched to 40-45 calorie bread per slice and haven't noticed a big difference. The slices are a little smaller but each piece is less than half the calories of traditional white bread)

¼ cup of 1% milk

2 tablespoons of sugar free maple syrup (this recipe changes to 5 SmartPoints per serving with regular syrup)

1 tablespoon of cinnamon

1 tablespoon of vanilla extract

Non-stick cooking spray

Step 1:

In a shallow mixing bowl, add the egg whites, milk, and vanilla extract. Whisk these ingredients together.

Step 2:

Coat a skillet with cooking spray and put it over low-medium heat. Dip both sides of your wheat bread into the mixing bowl from step 1 and add to the skillet. You should be able to cook roughly 2 pieces at a time.

Step 3:

While still hot, sprinkle cinnamon on each piece of toast. Serve with syrup and enjoy right away.

3 Minute Breakfast Mug – 2 SmartPoints Per Serving

Perhaps you thought 10 minutes was too long to dedicate to cooking a warm breakfast, well then this recipe is for you. This is a breakfast I used to make at the office as the ingredients can be stored easily in a refrigerator. You will absolutely need to use the liquid egg substitute as opposed to liquid eggs as the substitute will cook better in the microwave. If you have never used your microwave as a primary cooking tool, do not fear – this too was my first recipe cooked entirely in a microwave. When you get a look at the finished product you will be highly satisfied with the result – it tastes great too.

Ready in 3 Minutes

1 minute to prep and 2 minutes to cook

Ingredients (serves 1):

½ cup of liquid egg substitute

1 ounce of low-fat turkey breast (optional)

1 slice of American cheese

Non-stick cooking spray

Step 1:

Take a microwave-safe mug and coat it with the non-stick spray.

Step 2:

Pour the egg substitute into the mug and microwave on high for 1 minute.

Step 3:

Add in the cheese and optionally the turkey. If you're adding the turkey, you will want to make sure that it is in very fine pieces. Microwave for an additional minute.

Saturday Morning Enriching Oatmeal – 7 SmartPoints

This filling breakfast will have you thinking differently about oatmeal. We take a hearty essential oatmeal recipe and add a combination of zesty flavors that make the dish shine. This breakfast takes longer than the others to cook and is best enjoyed on a weekend, or when you have some extra time before starting your day. This recipe can easily be doubled or tripled to serve the entire family.

Ready in 30 Minutes

10 minutes to prep and 20 minutes to cook

Ingredients (serves 1):

½ cup raw oats

2 teaspoons of lemon juice

1/8 teaspoon of cinnamon

1/8 teaspoon of salt

1 low-calorie sweetener packet similar to Splenda

1 cup of unsweetened almond milk, or vanilla soy milk

1 cup of water

Step 1:

In a small pot, combine the oats, cinnamon, salt, almond milk, and water.

Step 2:

Heat the pot on high heat and bring the oatmeal to a near boil. Once bubbling reduce the heat to low. Cook for 10-15 minutes after the oatmeal has been put to low heat.

Step 3:

Stir occasionally and remove from burner when the oatmeal has thickened.

Step 4:

Before serving, add the sweetener packet to the serving bowl.

LUNCH RECIPES THAT WILL KEEP YOU SATISFIED ALL AFTERNOON

Home Joe's Mediterranean Hummus With Pita Bread – 4 Smart Points Per Serving

This recipe is based on a small love affair I have for the Trader Joe's Mediterranean Hummus. I have tweaked this recipe to get very much the same taste, but with all the added benefit of knowing exactly what ingredients are used. This hummus is packed full of healthy fats from the chick peas, fats that will leave you satisfied all afternoon. I love to bring a small container to work and pair it with either pita chips or pita bread and a side of fresh vegetables – carrots and peppers in particular. Be on the lookout for the nutritional information on the chips or pita bread of your choice – while the hummus is healthy, aim for a serving of less than 200 calories for whatever you choose to dip in the hummus and add 2 smart points to the meal. Feel free to use as many veggies as you want for dipping though, think about these as 0 points.

Ready in 30 Minutes

30 minutes to prepare.

Ingredients (serves 8):

A food processor that can hold 3 cups

1 large garlic glove

2 tablespoons of tahini

½ lemon

6 tablespoons of extra virgin olive oil (the taste is important here, so use extra virgin instead of "pure")

¼ teaspoon of cumin

1 teaspoon of crushed red pepper

½ cup of boiling water

Step 0:

This recipe is dependent on your food processor. You won't need to prepare any ingredients, but make sure that your processor is up to the task. I have had this recipe come out just a tad too lumpy in the past because of the food processor, so blending time may vary slightly to get the consistency that you want.

Step 1:

Put the garlic clove and the processor and pulse 3 to 4 times. Add the rest of the ingredients except for the water.

Step 2:

Run the processor for 3-5 minutes, periodically switching from pulse to long sustained processing.

Step 3:

Pour in the hot water (does not need to be exactly boiling) and run the processor for an additional 30 seconds to a minute. Check the consistency of the hummus and run the processor for additional time if needed. You may need to add more than ½ a cup of water depending in the consistency of the beans and how powerful your food processor is.

Step 4:

With the desired consistency, pour the hummus in to a container and store in the fridge for several hours. Serving right away will not yield the best flavor as the ingredients are still settling.

Step 5 (Optional):

If serving for a party or if you simply want slightly more indulgent hummus, add a drizzle of olive oil to the hummus before serving.

5 Minute Turkey Wrap – 8 SmartPoints Per Serving

I ate these wraps nearly three times a week for half a year – they were just that delicious. They're easy to make and great to bring as a bagged lunch.

Ready in 5 Minutes

5 minutes to prep and 0 minutes to cook

Ingredients (serves 1)

3 ounces of low-sodium turkey breast (I encourage you to use your local deli counter versus the prepackaged meats – the deli counter meats will often have less sodium so even if you aren't purchasing 'low-sodium' turkey, it is probably still worth it to buy from the deli counter)

1 ounce of lettuce or spinach

¼ of one whole tomato

1 tablespoon of low-fat ranch dressing

1 ounce of low-fat mozzarella cheese (you can use other cheeses, but for the calorie to size ratio, I find mozzarella to be the best investment)

1 wrap or flatbread that is between 100-150 calories per wrap/flatbread (your supermarket will have several options for you but I suggest the Flatout Wraps. These wraps are fluffy and delicious are only 90 calories. For wraps above 150 calories, add another SmartPoint to the recipe)

Step 1:

Take out your wrap or flatbread and heat it in the microwave for 15-20 seconds – this will fluff up your wrap and make it more malleable to shape.

Step 2:

Spread your low-fat ranch dressing over the wrap. Fill the wrap with your turkey, lettuce or spinach, tomatoes, and cheese.

Step 3:

Roll up your wrap and store for lunch or eat right away.

Slow Cooker Southern Style Chicken Soup -4 SmartPoints Per Serving

It's an all day affair that that will last you all week and then some. This hearty soup is great in the winter and full of exotic blends of flavors that will have you wondering why you don't eat soup more often. Since this recipe produces a fairly large batch, it's worth noting that this soup freezes extremely well. If you decide to freeze individual servings, simply let the soup thaw at room temperature before you reheat in the microwave – this is the best way to preserve the flavor.

Ready in 7 Hours

10 minutes to prep and 6-8 hours to cook

Ingredients (serves 10)

2 large chicken breasts cut into inch size cubes

1 clove of finely minced garlic

1 cup of corn (canned is what I use)

½ diced large white onion

½ cup of finely chopped chilantro

1 teaspoon of cumin

1 tablespoon of chili powder

15 ounces of washed and drained kidney beans (canned is what I use)

15 ounces of washed and drained black beans (canned is what I use)

1 teaspoon of lime juice

2 whole bell peppers cut into long strips

1 15 ounce can of diced tomatoes

Pepper to taste

Salt to taste

Step 1:

Prepare all of your ingredients and pour them into your slow cooker. Put the slow cookers on low heat and let cook for 6-8 hours. To make sure that the soup is done, reach for a piece of chicken and slice to find the color in the center. Note that it is very difficult to overcook this recipe – even 9 hours in the slow cooker will result in a fantastic soup.

Alternative: If you do not have a slow cooker, do not fret – a regular pot on low heat on your burner will do just fine. There are some limitations however in that you will need to be present the entire time the soup is cooking. It is also possible to overcook the soup if you are using a traditional pot (I first made this recipe using this method and it turned out great. It does require time and patience if you're using a pot, but it can be made over the weekend and enjoyed all week long).

Healthy Zone Calzone – 4 SmartPoints Per Serving

I love this recipe because it uses a neat trick – we substitute heavy dough for Pillsbury and get to cut down on the cooking time in the process. This dish is great by itself and works great as a lunch served at room temperature. If you decide to make the marinara sauce in the next chapter, try it as a dipping sauce for this delicious healthy calzone.

Ready in 40 Minutes

25 minutes to prep and 15 minutes to cook

Ingredients (serves 8):

1 can of reduced fat crescent rolls by Pillsbury (this is absolutely necessary to get the right amount of dough to calorie ratio)

¼ cup of reduce fat shredded cheese (mozzarella is my go to choice but feel free to use your favorite).

6 ounces of low-fat chicken breast

2 cups of baby spinach

6 tablespoons of low-fat whipped cream cheese (you can also use reduced fat but know that it changes the total SmartPoints per serving quite significantly).

1-2 tablespoons of vegetable oil

Step 1:

Take the chicken breast and cut it into cubes before cooking in a frying pan. Use the vegetable oil to cook the chicken and try to use the least amount of oil possible. This recipe is extremely lean and the vegetable oil is actually one of the more calorie expensive ingredients – any savings here do add up.

Step 2:

Preheat the oven to 375 degrees F or 190 degrees C.

Step 3:

Remove the Pillsbury rolls and arrange them on an ungreased baking tray. The container should contain 8 rolls but we are only making 4 calzones. Combine rolls to make the 4 calzones and make sure each roll is flat on the tray.

Step 4:

Spread over each roll the baby spinach, cream cheese, chicken, and your choice of shredded cheese. These rolls are fairly small for how stuffed these calzones will be (definitely a good thing), so you may need to kneed some of the ingredients into the dough itself – this works particularly well with the cream cheese and shredded cheese.

Step 5:

Form each of the individual 4 calzones, fold the dough over the ingredients and 'close' the calzone. This step can be a little tricky if the dough is not at room temperature. The final shape should look a little bit like a crescent moon

Step 6:

Bake for 10-15 minutes in the middle rack of the oven. You will know when the calzones are ready as the dough will begin to flake and turn brown.

8 Minute Tuna – 3 SmartPoints Per Serving

I still prepare this Tuna Salad at least twice a month. It's quick and easy and great to bring to work. If you feel like you're missing out on the pure indulgence of 'fatty' flavors then this salad will hit the spot. Even though we are using low-fat mayonnaise, it still hits all the right notes and you'd be hard pressed to tell the difference between this and a much more calorie dense mayonnaise base. One of the greatest aspects of this recipe, and why it's only 3 SmartPoints per serving, is the use of lettuce as the base for wraps.

We use lettuce for a couple of reasons: one, the neutral flavor of the lettuce brings out the creaminess of the salad without distorting the taste and two, the crispness of the lettuce is essential for the proper texture. I came up with the idea for using lettuce as a base after eating Korean barbeque. Try it and you'll see how it really does bring out the flavor.

Ready in 8 Minutes

8 minutes to prep and 0 minutes to cook

Ingredients (serves 4):

12 ounces of albacore white tuna in water (essential as this tuna has the meatiest texture and taste)

3 tablespoons of low-fat mayonnaise

3 stalks o chopped celery (if any part of the stalk is not hard, then do not use that section. You want the celery to be firm as to add a crunchiness to the salad).

1 teaspoon of Dijon mustard

½ teaspoon of black pepper

½ teaspoon of table-salt (do not use sea-salt as the harsher grain does not spread as evenly throughout the salad)

½ head of lettuce cut into large pieces (these will serve as the wraps for eating the tuna so keep that in mind as you cut the lettuce)

Step 1:

Drain the tuna and add to a large mixing bowl. Add the celery, pepper, salt, mustard, and mayonnaise. Stir well, breaking up the large pieces of tuna that might be sticking together from the can.

Step 2:

For best results, leave the salad in the fridge for 20 minutes to let thicken. Serve with the large pieces of lettuce.

Week-Long Rice With Chicken – 4 SmartPoints Per Serving

One of the essentials of preparing a good lunch is not having to worry about side dishes. This dish comes with everything you need – protein to keep you full, carbohydrates to give you afternoon energy, and veggies for your general nutrition and to flavor the dish. This rice dish can be stored away for work and can be enjoyed at room temperature or even cold – it will still taste delicious!

Ready in 30 Minutes

15 minutes to prep and 15 minutes to cook

Ingredients (serves 6):

2 large lean, boneless chicken breasts

2 large eggs

2 cups uncooked brown rice

½ cup of pea

½ cup of chopped carrots

2 finely chopped cloves of garlic

2 tablespoons of soy sauce (1 tablespoon if using low-sodium soy sauce – better results are gotten with regular soy)

4 tablespoons of water

Non-stick cooking spray or if unavailable, 1 tablespoon of vegetable oil

Step 1:

Take the chicken breast and cut the chicken into long strips. The important part of cutting the chicken is that each strip has roughly the same thickness. Do not worry about how thick or thin your chicken is – just make sure it is fairy uniform.

Step 2:

Cook the brown rice on your stovetop. Use 5 cups of water for the 2 cups of brown rice. This is more water than is typically used and you will need to cook the rice for slightly longer. The rice will fluff up much more with that extra cup of water. Move onto step 3 only after the rice is done.

Step 3:

In a large skillet, scramble the two large eggs and set aside.

Step 4:

Coat the same skillet again with non-stick cooking spray. Each skillet is a little bit difference and if you know that non-stick spray is not going to be able to grease the entire pan, use 1 tablespoon of vegetable oil, as we do not want the chicken to stick to the pan. Add the sliced chicken and cook halfway before adding the carrots. As the chicken starts to look fully cooked, add the chopped garlic and peas.

Step 4:

Take the soy sauce and pour it into a small dish with the water. Mix and pour into the skillet. The water will evaporate and ensure that the soy sauce is not too overpowering. Move onto step 5 once the chicken is fully cooked and the water is mostly evaporated.

Step 5:

Add into the skillet the cooked rice and scrambled eggs. Mix well and remove from the burner once the eggs have warmed up. Serve right away.

Admiral David's Broccoli – 5 SmartPoints Per Serving

If the name seems familiar, or just a bit off, that's because it is indeed a variation of General Tso's Chicken. It's a standard American Chinese dish that incorporates crisp chicken, spice, and a tinge of orange flavoring. This recipe is derived from a dish a college roommate of mine used to make. If you guessed his name is David, then you would be correct. As with many of the other lunch dishes, this one is also great when served cold. This dish is a complete meal and doubles as a fantastic dinner that is quick to make.

Ready in 25 Minutes

15 minutes to prep and 10 minutes to cook

Ingredients (serves 4):

2 large chicken breasts

1 orange, cut and peeled

1 teaspoon of corn starch

4 teaspoon of vegetable oil

1 bag of precut broccoli florets (should equal roughly 2 cups)

1 tablespoon of minced ginger

¼ cup water (to mix with soy sauce)

3 tablespoons of soy sauce

¼ cup of orange juice

½ cup of chicken or vegetable broth

½ cup water (for help in cooking broccoli)

Step 1:

Take the chicken breasts and cut into long strips. Add the soy sauce to the ¼ cup of water and mix, set aside. During this step, make sure that your other ingredients are all set and ready to go. Once the pan heats up the cooking processes is very fast.

Step 2:

Add the vegetable oil to a large skillet warm over medium heat. Add the chicken strips and cook halfway – add the ginger and continue to cook the chicken until it is entirely done. Take the chicken and ginger out of the skillet and set aside.

Step 3:

Return to the skillet and add the broccoli. You should not need to add any additional oil but if when removing the chicken the pan was left dry, add an additional teaspoon. As the broccoli starts to lightly brown add the ½ cup of water and cover the skillet. Let the broccoli steam for 3 minutes. Check the broccoli to make sure that it is cooked through and not too raw.

Step 4:

Add the cooked chicken and ginger to the skillet. Add the soy sauce mixed with water, the orange juice, and the chicken broth. Mix these ingredients well and allow to cook for an additional 5 minutes. If the chicken or broccoli is beginning to be overcooked, change the heat to low or turn off the burner.

Step 5:

Add in the cornstarch and continue to mix. Once the cornstarch has been mixed in, add the orange peels to the top of the dish and cook for an additional minute or two. Serve right away.

DINNER RECIPES FOR THE HEALTHY BODY

Lightning Fast Curry Noodles – 3 SmartPoints Per Serving

This is a recipe I commonly refer to when I'm looking to make a quick dinner with just a bit of Asian flair. My favorite aspect to this recipe is that by using rice noodles you do not need to cook the noodles in a pot of boiling water. It can be made with just about any protein, including eggs or tofu. This particular version is vegetarian free, but adding cooked chicken or beef works just as well. This is my own recipe is supposed to mimic Singapore Noodles, a dish commonly found at Chinese restaurants throughout the country.

Ready In 20 Minutes:

10 minutes to prepare and 10 minutes to cook

Ingredients (serves 4)

3 large eggs

2 tablespoons whole milk (or half and half)

3 teaspoons of curry powder

2 tablespoons of vegetable oil

2 whole white mushrooms

1 bell pepper

1 package of Rice Noodles (you will want to go for medium thickness in the noodle – the particular brand does not matter)

2 tablespoons of soy sauce (low sodium soy sauce will *taste* more salty than regular soy sauce. If using low sodium soy then only use 1 tablespoon)

Step 1:

Take a large bowl or pot and fill it with warm water. The water does not need to approach boiling, and running hot water from your tap will suffice. Once the bowl is full, put the package of rice noodles into the water. You want to check back in a few minutes to make sure that every noodle is submerged in the water.

Step 2:

Slice the mushrooms and bell peppers into small slices. This dish will look a lot like a noodle stir fry, so cut the peppers in long strips and the mushrooms into thin slices.

Step 3:

While the noodles are soaking, use a small frying pan and with the milk and 3 eggs, make scrambled eggs. Once the eggs are made put them aside on a separate plate and cut the scrambled eggs into small pieces.

Step 4:

As the eggs are cooking, take a pan suitable for stir fry and add the vegetable oil. If you do not have a suitable stir fry pan, you can also use a standard pot for boiling pasta. Bring the heat to medium high and once the oil is hot add the mushrooms. As the mushrooms start to cook, add the peppers.

Step 5:

Strain the rice and noodles and add them to the pan with the mushrooms and the bell peppers. Note that the noodles should still appear to be a little bit brittle, do not worry as they will continue to cook in the pan.

Step 6:

As the noodles are cooking in the pan, add the soy sauce and mix thoroughly. Once the sauce is mixed, add the curry powder and stir thoroughly. The noodles should start to take on a dark yellowish color and at this point they should be thoroughly cooked through.

Step 7:

Add the cooked eggs to the pan, and then serve immediately. If the scrambled eggs are slightly cold, they will be warmed up through the cooked noodles.

Step 8:

Serve immediately and enjoy! This meal also works great for lunch. If you are unable to reheat the noodles while at work, they taste great just at room temperature.

Simple Season Chicken– 3 SmartPoints Per Serving

This recipe is a great healthy way to make seasoned chicken cutlets. These cutlets have just the right amount of seasoning and come packed with all the healthy protein of lean chicken breast. This recipe can altered slightly to make a lean type of chicken parmesan. See the altered steps 4 and 5 if you wish to go this route, otherwise this recipe is great with a side of spinach or any other side vegetable.

Ready In 35 Minutes

10 minutes to prepare and 25 minutes to cook

Ingredients (serves 4)

Chicken breast (use roughly 1 pound and cut into 4 large filets)

1/8 teaspoon paprika

¼ cup of parmesan cheese (grated finely)

½ teaspoon of garlic powder

1 teaspoon of parsley (optional)

black pepper to taste

3 tablespoons of dried breadcrumbs

Directions:

Step 1:

Preheat your oven to 400 degrees F or 205 degrees C

Step 2:

Take a small mixing bowl and add the breadcrumbs, grated parmesan, garlic powder, and paprika. Add a pinch of black pepper but know that you can add more while the chicken is cooking.

Step 3:

Take your sliced pieces of chicken breast and dip them into the bowl. Coat both sides of each piece of chicken. Since we are using a healthier version of traditional chicken parmesan, you might have some difficult having the mix stick to the chicken. It is best dip the chicken in the bowl right after you wash the chicken, using the moisture to get it to stick properly.

Step 4:

Prepare a nonstick baking tray and align the pieces of chicken towards the center of the baking tray.

Alternate for Chicken Parmesan: Using the Homemade Multi-Purpose Marina sauce (the next recipe in the book), lather the chicken liberally in 2-3 cups of sauce. You will need to use a deeper baking dish to cook the Chicken Parmesan. Once the sauce and chicken has been laid out, coat with shredded Parmesan Cheese and whole slices of mozzarella. To use an appropriate amount of cheese, only layer the cheese on top of the chicken filets. Note that this adds roughly 2 Smart Points to each serving.

Step 5:

Let the chicken bake in the oven for 25 minutes. Check at about 20 minutes as thinner pieces of chicken will cook more quickly. 25 minutes is around the upper limit for how long it will take to cook the chicken.

Alternate for Chicken Parmesan: Using the oven set to 400 degrees F, bake for 35-40 minutes.

Step 6: Remove the chicken form the baking tray and serve within 5-10 minutes.

Homemade Multi-Purpose Marinara – 3 Smart Points Per Serving

This is a great recipe to try out on the weekend and use all week long. Whether it's topping for Chicken Parmesan, dipping sauce for bread, or the foundation of a great pasta dish, this marinara sauce will leave you with plenty of options for how to enjoy it.

Ready in 30 Minutes

10 minutes to prepare and 20 minutes to cook

Ingredients (makes 1 quart)

2 large cloves of garlic

4 large tomatoes

1 28 ounce can of peeled tomatoes

3 tablespoons of olive oil (use extra virgin olive oil – the taste will make a huge difference)

1 ½ tablespoons of sugar

½ teaspoon of ground black pepper

1 teaspoon of salt

½ large white onion

Step 1:

Take your fresh tomatoes and dice them into small chunks. You can also optionally peel the skin from the tomatoes for a smoother sauce. During this step also chop your half onion and your garlic cloves.

Step 2:

In large sauce pan, heat the olive oil under a medium heat, add the diced onion. Wait until the onion is firmly sautéing before adding the garlic.

Step 3:

Add your chopped tomatoes and your can of tomatoes. Also stir in your black pepper and salt. Bring the heat up to medium high and wait for the sauce to boil. Stir frequently and let the sauce boil for 15 minutes.

Step 4:

Turn the heat down to low on the burner and let the sauce simmer for an additional 30 minutes.

Savory Grilled Salmon – 4 Smart Points Per Serving

If there's a common theme with this cookbook, it's the idea that healthy proteins are the foundation to a great diet. Even if you do not normally love salmon, or if you've never tried it, this recipe is certainly worth a shot. At 4 SmartPoints per serving, a side dish of potatoes and spinach will bring the total meal to a reasonable 6-7 SmartPoints, meanwhile the salmon will keep you full until morning.

Ready in 50 Minutes

30 minutes to prep and 20 minutes to cook

Ingredients (serves 4):

1 pound of skinless salmon fillet. You will want the thickness of the salmon to be about 1 inch.

¼ cup of soy sauce

Non-stick cooking spray

1 tablespoon of rice wine vinegar

¼ cup of dry sherry

1 tablespoon of brown sugar

1 teaspoon of garlic powder

1/8 teaspoon of ginger

Black pepper to taste

Step 1:

Preheat the oven to 375 degrees F or 190 degrees C. Make sure the grill rack is in the center of the oven.

Step 2:

Combine the sherry, soy sauce, brown sugar, vinegar, garlic powder, and ginger in a mixing bowl.

Step 3:

Dip the filets of salmon in the mixing bowl and place in the refrigerator for 20 minutes to marinade.

Step 4:

Place the remaining marinade in a small saucepan and heat on low. The marinade will begin to thicken as the salmon marinades in the refrigerator.

Step 5:

Spray the grill rack with non-stick spray and place the salmon filets on the rack. The cooking time for the salmon will differ greatly depending on thickness. As a guideline each side will need 4 to 8 minutes to cook through. The sign that the salmon is fully cooked is when it begins to flake.

Step 6:

Remove the salmon from the oven and place it on a large serving plate. Coat the salmon in the remaining marinade. Serve immediately.

Cheesy Baked Chicken – 5 SmartPoints Per Serving

I love this dish if for no other reason than it remind me that dieting does not need to omit cream and cheese. This chicken dish has all the flavor of a delicious casserole without any of the guilt. A simple side dish like a lightly tossed salad goes great, just be sure not to overdo it with the dressing.

Ready in 55 minutes:

10 minutes to prep and 45 minutes to cook

Ingredients (serves 8):

2 cups of cooked macaroni noodles

2 cups of 1% fat skin milk

2 cups of chopped boneless chicken breasts cut into cubes

8 ounces of low-fat shredded cheddar cheese

2 cups of undiluted cream of mushroom soup (I personally use Campbell's brand)

Step 1:

Preheat the oven to 350 degrees F or 175 degrees C.

Step 2:

Use a baking dish that is 2 inches deep, similar to a casserole dish, and place the cream of mushroom soup, the skim milk, cooked macaroni, shredded cheese, and uncooked chicken breasts into the baking tray. Mix thoroughly.

Step 3:

Place the baking tray in the center oven rack and bake for 35 minutes. At 35 minutes, take the baking tray out of the oven and remove a piece of chicken. Cut the chicken in half to see if it is cooked all the way through. Typically this recipe calls for 45 minutes, but if the chicken pieces are small enough the dish could be done in 35. Cook for an additional 10 minutes if needed.

Step 4:

45 minutes is the upper limit for cooking the casserole, but always make sure to slice the chicken and make sure that it is cooked all the way through. Small variables could mean cooking for an additional 5-10 minutes.

Step 5:

Let the dish cook for 10 minutes before serving.

Lean Mean Pork Chops – 3 SmartPoints Per Serving

In this recipe we are using our oven to bypass the unnecessary oil we'd get in by using a frying pan. This will lead to a more brazen pork that should be more tender. This dish takes longer than several of our other dinners and so use this time to experiment with side dishes. A vegetable melody goes great as the extra time gives you the opportunity to wash and cut your vegetables. You can also use the already heated oven for simple sliced baked potatoes – even the spices from the pork can be reused if you wish.

Ready in 70 Minutes

20 minutes to prep and 50 minutes to cook

Ingredients Needed (serves 4):

Non-stick cooking spray

1 large egg white

¼ teaspoon of ground ginger

1/8 teaspoon of garlic powder

2 tablespoon of pineapple juice

6 ounces of pork loin (try and get lean pork if available)

1 tablespoon of soy sauce

¼ teaspoon of paprika

1/3 cup dried breadcrumbs

¼ teaspoon of dried Italian seasoning

Step 1:

Preheat the oven to 350 degrees F or 175 degrees C

Step 2:

If you were able to purchase lean pork loin then you do not need to follow this step. If you were not able to purchase lean pork loin, trim away as much fat as you can. Do not worry about the taste – our seasoning will make up for the flavor.

Step 3:

In large mixing bowl, add the soy sauce, garlic powder, egg white, ginger, and pineapple juice. Mix well as the egg white is sometimes difficult to mix thoroughly.

Step 4:

Using a separate bowl, mix breadcrumbs, Italian seasoning, and the paprika.

Step 5:

Take the pork chops and dip them into the wet mixing bowl and then dip them into the dry mixing bowl. Coat the pork chops well but know that some ingredients will be left.

Step 6:

Lay the pork chops on the baking tray. Bake for 25-30 minutes on each side. Wait 3-5 minutes before serving.

Fast Cooking Scallops – 3 SmartPoints Per Serving

The hardest part of this recipe is the trip to the supermarket to purchase scallops. Do not fear as frozen scallops will work just fine, and if you are inexperienced cooking fish you also do not have to worry – this recipe is built upon the idea that perhaps this is your first time cooking fish in a pan. If you are unsure about whether to try this recipe, think about scallops as the 'meatier' shrimp. For a side dish, I recommend a baked potato and spinach or zucchini. The lemon goes great with subtle side dishes like these.

Ready in 20 Minutes

10 minutes to prep and 10 minutes to cook

Ingredients (serves 4):

1 pound of sea scallops, dried

2 tablespoons of all purpose flour

1 tablespoon of virgin olive oil

1 tablespoon of lemon juice

1 minced scallions

¼ teaspoon of salt

2 tablespoons of parsley

Pinch of sage (nice flavor, but not necessary if you don't already have this spice)

Step 1:

Take a mixing bowl and add the flour, scallions, and salt.

Step 2:

Take the scallops and dip them in the mixing bowl. Don't worry about how much of the mix ends up on the scallions – it should only be a small layer and does not necessary need to cover the scallops entirely.

Step 3:

Take a large skillet and heat the olive oil under medium heat. Toss the scallops one at a time into the pan. The scallops should could in about 4 minutes. Be careful not to overcook the scallops as they will become very though. You will know the scallops are done when they become impossible to see through the skin.

Step 4:

If the scallops were made in batches, add all of the scallops back into the pan, turning off the heat before you do so. Add the chopped parsley and lemon juice. Mix well and serve right away

CPSIA information can be obtained
at www.ICGtesting.com
Printed in the USA
LVHW021214121120
671417LV00014B/2030